PLURALISMS AND HORIZONS

Pluralisms and Horizons

An Essay in Christian Public Philosophy

Richard Mouw

⟶ and ⟵

Sander Griffioen

William B. Eerdmans Publishing Company
Grand Rapids, Michigan

Library of Congress Cataloging-in-Publication Data

Griffioen, S., 1941-
Pluralisms and horizons: an essay in Christian public philosophy /
Sander Griffioen and Richard J. Mouw.
p.   cm.
Includes bibliographical references and index.
ISBN 0-8028-0658-9 (pbk.)
1. Sociology, Christian. 2. Pluralism (Social sciences)
3. Christian ethics — Reformed authors.
I. Mouw, Richard J. II. Title.
BT738.G727 1993
261'.1 — dc20   92-21465
                                                        CIP

. . . *true democracy begins*
With free confession of our sins.
In this alone we are all the same,
All are so weak that none dare claim
"I have the right to govern," or
"Behold in me the Moral Law,"
And all real unity commences
In consciousness of differences . . .

— W. H. Auden

Contents

Acknowledgments

THIS STUDY began in the early 1980s when three institutions sharing common roots in the Reformed tradition — the Vrije Universiteit of Amsterdam, Calvin College in Grand Rapids, Michigan, and Toronto's Institute for Christian Studies — agreed to foster collaborative projects in social theory. Generous funding from the Provost of Calvin College and the Rector and Philosophy Department of the Vrije Universiteit, and at a later point from Fuller Theological Seminary, made it possible for the two of us to pursue our interests together for extended periods of time in both the Netherlands and the United States.

Scott Flipse, research assistant in the Office of the Provost at Fuller Seminary, skillfully performed a number of valuable tasks in preparing the manuscript for publication. Special thanks must also be offered to our wives, Dorine Griffioen and Phyllis Mouw, for their sacrificial support — demonstrated in ways too numerous to detail here — for this project.

Pluralism in Perspective

IN SEPTEMBER of 1983 a group of scholars interested in the current status of social scientific theorizing met for a few days at the University of Chicago to discuss "Potentialities for Knowledge in Social Science." When Donald Fiske and Richard Shweder prepared the published volume of the papers presented at this conference, they chose to supplement the rather forbidding title *Metatheory in Social Sciences* with this intriguing subtitle: *Pluralisms and Subjectivities*.

This was an appropriate amplification. The essays devote much attention to the lack of consensus among social scientists on rather basic issues. Many of the Chicago conferees could remember a time when a mood of optimism prevailed in the social sciences about the possibility of achieving a "unified science" in the study of humankind. But they are now very much aware, as Fiske and Shweder describe their mood, of "the persistence, even entrenchment, of multiple paradigms or schools of thought and the lack of convergence over time in the theories and concepts that guide research and are used to interpret evidence"; these days "no reduction seems to be occurring in the diversity of conceptualizations and higher-order theories, and many basic issues never seem to get resolved."[1]

Social scientists are not the only people in contemporary life who are finding "pluralisms and subjectivities" something with which they must reckon. We are all very aware these days of competing and apparently irreconcilable points of view in many arenas of human interaction. Indeed, the list of items about which there is an important lack of convergence seems almost endless: sexual orientations, religious perspectives, family life-styles, ideas about justice, visions of peace, theories of human origins, definitions of human health and happiness, and so on.

To be sure, human disagreement is nothing new. It has been around for a long time, and the chronicles of scholarly reflection show that intelligent people have always viewed it as an important matter for their attention.

But some thinkers today argue that the experience of divergence is formative in a very special way in contemporary life; the intense awareness of pluralities, they say, is a distinctive mark of modernity. As Max Stackhouse puts the case: "Perhaps no societies in the history of humanity have been as pluralistic and dynamic as modern ones. Indeed, the terms 'pluralistic' and 'dynamic' have become not only descriptive of the ways things are but prescriptive of the way things ought to be."[2]

Not everyone would agree with Stackhouse's thesis as stated. Some scholars believe that the experience of "deep" pluralism is an illusion; they argue that while a lack of

---

1. Donald W. Fiske and Richard A. Shweder, eds., *Metatheory in Social Science: Pluralisms and Subjectivities* (Chicago: University of Chicago Press, 1986), 5.

2. Max L. Stackhouse, *Public Theology and Political Economy: Christian Stewardship in Modern Society* (Grand Rapids, MI: Wm. B. Eerdmans Publishing Co. for Commission on Stewardship, National Council of the Churches of Christ in the U.S.A., 1987), 157.

convergence does seem quite obvious on the surface of our culture, on a more basic level modern cultural life is actually becoming increasingly monolithic. Others would agree that pluralism is an accurate description of the way things are, but not an adequate prescription for the way things ought to be.

There is much of importance to consider in such arguments. But Stackhouse is surely correct in insisting that the experiences of the "pluralistic" and the "dynamic" are important elements in the consciousness of many people today. Fiske and Shweder point out, for example, that while not all social scientists are deeply troubled by the seemingly deep divisions that characterize the theoretical *status quo* in their disciplines, they agree on at least this point: "Whether or not one is troubled by those things, they are the kinds of things with which one must come to terms, especially if one is concerned with the potentialities for the growth of knowledge in the social sciences."[3]

The conviction that pluralities are the kinds of things with which one must come to terms can also be observed on the broader cultural canvas. Celebrating basic diversities has been a constant theme in recent Western culture, even though the popular language used to celebrate differences ("do your own thing"; "different strokes for different folks") is subject to periodic change.

PLURALISM AND CHRISTIAN CONVICTION

It is not uncommon to find people arguing that Christian belief is simply incompatible with tolerating pluralities in public life. This seems to be Donald Atwell Zoll's assessment when, for example, he argues in his book *Twentieth Century*

3. Fiske and Shweder, *Metatheory in Social Science,* 4; see also 364-367.

Political Philosophy that any attempt to show that Christianity and democratic theory are compatible is "fraught with philosophical difficulties, not the least of which is the obligation to show how religious eschatology is reconcilable with the relativistic, appetitive foundations of popular democratic thought."[4] Whatever else Zoll might be getting at in this remark, at least this much is clear: he is convinced that people who believe that their perspective on life will be vindicated in the end-time have problems getting along in the kind of political society that encourages the toleration of diverse viewpoints.

And it is certainly not difficult to find evidence for Zoll's claim. The history of Christian thought and practice provides us with an abundance of examples of Christians who would be happy to second Zoll's thesis that the attempt to reconcile the possession of strong Christian beliefs with the toleration of diverse perspectives is "fraught with philosophical difficulties."

Nor would Zoll need to confine his attention to rigid traditionalists in gathering support for his contention from within the religious community. Union Seminary professor Tom Driver has recently argued that we have no hope of ridding the world of the vestiges of political Constantinianism — the practice of requiring everyone else to conform to our standards of public behavior — unless we Christians are also willing to divest ourselves of our theological Constantinianism, that is, the "old habit of supposing that in matters of salvation and liberation there is only one true way."[5]

The 19th- and 20th-century missionary movement, Driver

4. Donald Atwell Zoll, *Twentieth Century Political Philosophy* (Englewood Cliffs, N.J.: Prentice-Hall, 1974), 94.
5. Tom F. Driver, "Toward a Theocentric Christology," *Christianity and Crisis* 45, no. 18 (Nov. 11, 1985): 450.

contends, can in one sense be viewed as "a last great heave of the Constantinian spirit before its demise, although it may also be viewed without contradiction as Western Christianity's unwitting preparation for an age of interaction among the world's many religions and cultures" — a period of a new kind of religious egalitarianism in which "the main principle of political (and hence ecclesiastical) morality has already become not the centralization of political or ecclesiastical power but the dispersal of it into a genuine pluralism of interests, powers, and convictions."[6]

Driver would agree with the intolerant Christians of the past (and the present!) in their insistence that strong religious truth-claims do not sit well with a spirit of toleration. However, while Constantinian Christians have concluded that they have no alternative but to oppose toleration, Driver advocates the abandonment of strong truth-claims. Rejecting theological Constantinianism means for him that Christians must come "to regard the faith and truth of other religions as of an equal validity to their own."[7]

Driver is right to condemn the intolerance and the oppression that have permeated Constantinian programs, whether political or theological. But a thoroughgoing egalitarian approach to religious teachings will strike many Christians as much too high a price to pay in our efforts to avoid the Constantinian spirit. For some of us the real challenge is to eschew Constantinianism while continuing to embrace the unique truth-claims of the gospel.

Still, Driver has to be taken seriously when he takes it for granted that this is no easy assignment. The sociologist John Murray Cuddihy nicely captures the difficulties of the challenge in the title for one of his books on the subject of

6. Ibid.
7. Ibid.

religious toleration: *The Ordeal of Civility*. Cuddihy intends no exaggeration. Civility demands that we display tact, niceness, moderation, refinement, good manners — all the stuff that the modernization project requires of people who want to be thought of as "civilized."[8] And Cuddihy is well aware of those forces, indigenous to Judaism and Christianity, that compel believers to resist this requirement that they divest themselves of any sense of "sacred particularity."[9] He quotes approvingly Rabbi Arthur Hertzberg's observation that "the American experiment" has asked "something previously unknown and almost unthinkable of the religions," namely, that "each sect is to remain the one true and revealed faith for itself and in private, but each must *behave in the public arena as if* its truth were as tentative as an esthetic opinion or a scientific theory."[10]

Cuddihy is right to suggest that trying to conform to these expectations has the character of an ordeal. In the final analysis, though, he does think that the ordeal can result in a civility that does not require sacrificing conviction. Indeed, on his analysis, a primary biblical resource for surviving the ordeal of civility is the eschatological vision: people of conviction can cultivate civility, he argues, if they can convince themselves that the "perfect community" will appear only at "the end of time."[11] Interestingly, Cuddihy appeals here to the very area of theology that Zoll views as the major source of those "philosophical difficulties" that plague any attempt to reconcile Christianity with democratic thought. We will return to Cuddihy's proposal in a later chapter.

8. John Murray Cuddihy, *The Ordeal of Civility: Freud, Marx, Levi-Strauss, and the Jewish Struggle with Modernity* (Boston: Beacon Press, 1987), 235.
9. Ibid.
10. John Murray Cuddihy, *No Offense: Civil Religion and Protestant Taste* (New York: The Seabury Press, A Crossroad Book, 1978), 108.
11. Ibid., 210-211.

6

PLURALISMS AND HORIZONS

When Franz von Baader delivered the convocation address at the University of Munich in 1826, he bemoaned the decay of cultural unity, decrying the "anarchy of opinions" and the "spiritual deluge" of doctrinal confusion that he saw around him. Nonetheless, he did not view this increasing pluralism in purely negative terms. Drawing on the resources of his own Roman Catholic piety, Baader saw some sort of light at the end of the tunnel: the cultural darkness that was descending, he speculated, was the crisis that would prepare the world for a more glorious manifestation of God. Baader even hinted that it was, on his reading of the situation, the very diversity of the present that would serve to cast the coming glory into bolder relief.[12]

Whether Baader was aware of it or not, his comments had a close affinity to the views expressed by Hegel in the final passages of *Faith and Knowledge.* Hegel also evaluates contemporary plurality in the light of a *kairos* of expectation. The rise of modern subjectivism with its concomitant spread of unbelief, Hegel argues, is a "universal Good Friday," a necessary crisis preparing the way for the final outpouring of the Spirit on all flesh, an eschaton in which diversity will be preserved in a larger unity.[13]

What Baader and Hegel are offering is a metaperspective on pluralism. They are depicting a horizon against which we can see the overall shape of a particular kind of plurality, so as better to understand its place in the scheme of things. To offer a strong defense of, or an attack upon,

---

12. See Hans Grassl, "Franz Xaver von Baader," in *Unbekanntes Bayern, Portraets aus acht Jahrhunderten,* vol. 3 (Muenchen: Süddeutscher Verlag, 1975), 195.

13. Georg W. F. Hegel, *Faith and Knowledge,* trans. Walter Cerf and H. S. Harris (Albany, N.Y.: State University of New York Press, 1977), 189-191.

some kind of pluralistic pattern is often to invite us to see that plurality against a larger metaphysical-epistemological backdrop.

To be sensitive to this fact is to realize that not everyone who defends pluralism is in fact espousing a thoroughgoing relativism, even when the person seems at first glance to be pointing approvingly to deep differences in, for example, "ways of knowing." Often what is being endorsed is only a rather limited plurality. The endorser actually operates with fairly clear criteria for deciding what is or is not to be included within the pluralism in question.

Take Tom Driver's claim, already quoted, that we have experienced a "dispersal" of political and ecclesiastical power "into a genuine pluralism of interests, powers, and convictions." If Driver really does mean to be espousing a thoroughgoing relativism in making this claim, then he is saying that we have arrived at a time in history when it is no longer legitimate for people to appeal to any norm or standard in arguing that one interest or power or conviction is more reasonable or plausible than any other. If this is his meaning, though, he can hardly insist that the claims associated with political or theological Constantinianism are false or poorly grounded. He would have to say instead that the varieties of Constantinianism have no less a right to be espoused than various rival claims.

Yet Driver obviously does think that there are good grounds for rejecting various Constantinian claims. Indeed, when he gives examples of the pluralistic trends increasingly manifested in our culture, he explicitly tells us that Constantinians — even though they continue to be prominent — need no longer be taken seriously: "Monster-mouthed and ferocious as the Christian reactionaries may be, the evidence against their persuasiveness is mounting, which may help to explain their bellicosity." By way of contrast, Driver lauds the existence of a single pot in which stir the radical voices of liberation theology, feminist theology, Black Afro-American theology, Black African theology, Asian Christian theology, Amerindian theology, and more. The "pot" holding these together is the conviction that the Constantinian age is over, deprived already of any moral or theological justification it might ever have had, and due in good time to exit the world stage.[14]

Driver clearly has not given up on making evaluations about which particular claims, among those set forth from a plurality of diverse perspectives, are more or less reasonable. He thinks that Constantinian claims are no longer "persuasive," that they lack "any moral or theological justification," whereas a stew of various alternative perspectives is actually held together by a correct consensus-conviction regarding the inadequacy of Constantinian thought.

Driver is in fact placing limits on a thoroughgoing relativism — even if only implicitly — in favoring the specific perspectives he is highlighting here. Such limits are necessary if we are to take these perspectives seriously. No relativist viewpoint could really do justice to the points of view that he actually mentions. At the heart of what is being said by the theological "voices" that Driver commends to us is the claim that important experiences which have been systematically ignored by ecclesiastical and theological elites in the past — the experiences of black slaves and Native Americans, for example — have a right to be taken seriously. This sense that previously ignored viewpoints have something that ought to be given due consideration cannot be accounted for by a relativistic pluralism.

Still, a relativist might argue that Constantinian and non-Constantinian viewpoints cannot in fact coexist in a common political framework — that any society must decide for one

14. Driver, "Theocentric," 450.

or the other. But if there really are no standards of reasonable-ness or plausibility to be appealed to in evaluating the competing perspectives, the choice is finally reduced to one of power. Despite Driver's professed optimism about the direction of human history, it is not at all clear that the non-Constantinian political schemes will win out in such a struggle. And when we are also deprived of the normative grounds for saying that the political Constantinians *ought* to lose, the situation is an unhappy one.

Yet it seems obvious that Driver does not really intend to move us in that relativistic direction. He wants to encourage a rich diversity of perspectives on one level of consideration, while pointing to a horizon, a metaphysical-epistemological backdrop, against which it becomes possible to sort out and to discern what is "really" going on at the level of diversity. Thus his insistence that the liberationist and ethnic voices he is commending coexist in a "pot" that is held together by common anti-Constantinian conviction. Driver's discussion il-lustrates the fact that one can strongly affirm pluralism without thereby endorsing an ultimate relativism.

CROSS-CULTURAL COMPARISONS

The importance of maintaining clarity about this distinction between these two levels of discussion — a lower-order rec-ognition of plurality and a higher-order depiction of a horizon against which that plurality can be understood — is high-lighted in the cross-cultural explorations of Bryan Wilson, Martin Hollis, Steven Lukes, Ernest Gellner, and others.[15] Suppose someone argues, for example, that there are no

15. See the essays collected in *Rationality,* Key Concepts in the Social Sciences, Bryan R. Wilson, ed. (Oxford: Basil Blackwell, 1970), and *Ratio-nality and Relativism,* ed. Martin Hollis and Steven Lukes (Oxford: Basil Blackwell, 1982).

norms for deciding between the kind of "explanation" prof-
fered by Zande witches and the explanatory schemes provided by Western scientists. Any effort to show that Western
science is more "rational" than Zande witchcraft will appeal
to standards — such as the ability to make predictions in
efficient ways — which are themselves dependent upon
Western conceptions of rationality and alien to Zande patterns
of thought. Such cross-cultural evaluations, the argument
goes, are really exercises in cultural imperialism: in this case
the standards of North Atlantic Enlightenment thought are
being arbitrarily foisted upon people for whom those standards are alien.

People who offer such arguments often fail to see that
they have already gone well beyond what is permitted by a
straightforward relativism. They are suggesting, for example,
that what is being offered by the non-Westerner is an "explanation," or that what we are faced with between the two
efforts are different "standards," or that there are cross-cultural
standards for deciding what is "alien" to a cultural experience.
Acknowledging these considerations, however, does not simply end the discussion. Steven Lukes, for one, admits to the
importance of these concerns while remaining "partially se-
duced by the thought that the goodness — the strength and
relevance — of reasons for belief can depend on culture and
context."[16] But the very fact that Lukes is only partially
tempted by this way of viewing things indicates that he is
committed to a meta-level discussion in which cross-cultural
sense can be made of such notions as "relevance" and
"cultural-dependency." A thoroughgoing relativism regarding
such matters would seem to require a rather quick retreat
into silence.

Such silence would not only be tragic because of its
concession that the choice among perspectives competing

16. Hollis and Lukes, *Rationality and Relativism*, 11.

11

for the ability to regulate our communal lives must finally be decided by power alone. It would also be a serious loss for those groups who would thereby once again be denied a voice in the human dialogue. One of the more intriguing features of contemporary appeals for cultural pluralism is that they often involve a serious request — as we have seen in Driver's comments — that we listen carefully to long-ignored voices: the pleadings of the powerless and marginalized, and the testimonies of peoples whose visions and hopes have often been rejected as "primitive" and "superstitious." Those voices would, it is feared, once again be drowned out in a world wherein relativistic pluralism took hold as the ultimate assessment of human diversity. Such a world would suffer from a mood that Max Stackhouse describes well in these perceptive comments:

> The view that nothing could be true or right or good in any constant or knowable way, that everything depends on the immediate demands of the situation and on the perspective from which we see it, does indeed lead to a kind of dynamic pluralism. But it is a pluralism that surely cannot guide our thought or our lives in the cosmopolitan world of modern political economy. It implies that no vision of God, humanity, or the world could be judged to be any more valid than any other view, and that what we have is some passing opinion or contextual eruption that has no claim on us and for which no warrants could be given.[17]

This is not an attractive state of affairs. And, as we have been arguing, we would be missing something important in many defenses of pluralism if we thought that their design would lead us into this kind of normlessness. Indeed, defenders of pluralism are often intent upon de-

17. Stackhouse, *Public Theology*, 159.

12

stroying older unities only because they nurture the hope that more appropriate unities will eventually take their place. This was Hegel's meaning when he depicted the emergence of a new pluralistic subjectivism as a "Good Friday"; Hegel was happy to see the destruction of the older Constantinian-style unity of belief because he was convinced that only a Good Friday despair could give rise to the unity-in-diversity of a post-Easter Pentecost. He could celebrate the fact of increasing pluralism precisely because he viewed that pluralism against a more distant horizon in which unity is a dominant feature.

ABOUT "PLURALISMS"

Thus far we have been referring in a rather indiscriminate fashion to a wide variety of pluralisms. It is time now to become more disciplined in our discussion, since our primary focus in this book is on those pluralisms that figure prominently in discussions of public life.

Of course, there is something to be gained in the study of specific pluralisms from an investigation of pluralisms in general. Even though we cannot offer an exhaustive investigation along those lines here, a few brief comments are in order on the taxonomy of pluralisms.

A "pluralism" is an "ism" about a "plurality." In this sense a pluralistic account gets set forth when someone is convinced that there is something important to say about a given "manyness." This construal fits the "many" of the facts of usage. People often start talking about pluralism when some plurality strikes them as a phenomenon that needs attending to. When a journalist writes an article on "sexual pluralism," she does so because she is convinced that sexual "manyness" is a phenomenon that deserves attention. Likewise, scholarly discourses on "religious pluralism" mean to highlight the significance of the existence of a diversity of religious orientations.

Not all pluralities get "isms" attached to them, of course. There are, for example, many purple things in the universe, as well as many different freckle shapes. But little has been made to date of, say, a "purple pluralism" or a "freckle-shape pluralism." Pluralisms come into being when specific pluralities take on a special significance for a person or group.

The significance attached to a given plurality can fall into one of two categories. The pluralism label is sometimes used as a means of *advocating* diversity. We can think of this as the *normative* sense of the term. People who talk about "sexual pluralism," for example, want everyone to see the existence of diverse sexual preferences and practices as a good state of affairs. A person might even describe himself as a pluralist when he is calling for a diversity that does not yet exist, as when someone advocates doctrinal pluralism in a conservative denomination that is presently very homogeneous in its theology.

The pluralist label, however, can also be used in a *descriptive* sense, not necessarily as a means of advocating that diversity, but simply as a way of *acknowledging* its existence as a fact that is worth noting. Someone might refer to the moral pluralism of her society in the course of calling for a return to a single set of "moral absolutes." Here she subscribes to pluralism only in the sense that she admits that there is indeed a plurality that must be reckoned with, even if the reckoning takes the form of denouncing that plurality.

Descriptive pluralisms are usually less controversial than the normative variety. People who advocate normative pluralisms are not always themselves very clear about what they are advocating. There are people who insist, for example, that all sexual orientations, as long as they seem "natural" to the people possessing them, ought to be treated as equally legitimate. From their illustrations it is usually clear that the

14

sexual orientations they have in mind have to do with such patterns as promiscuous heterosexual and homosexual behavior, extramarital affairs, and the use of pornography. But do they also mean to include rape, incest, necrophilia, and bestiality? Some defenders of sexual pluralism seem reluctant to extend their tolerance to all of these patterns. If they do want to draw the line with these cases, then their normative pluralism is of a "contained" sort.

Arguments about descriptive pluralisms are more likely to focus on questions regarding the degree of plurality that is being claimed. People who argue, for example, that all homosexuals are persons who have chosen to distort or suppress their "natural" heterosexuality are obviously trying to minimize the degree of "real" sexual plurality that exists. Later on we will consider a similar attempt to minimize normative religious pluralism with the insistence that the North American religious situation is not as diverse as it is sometimes claimed to be.

PUBLIC PLURALITIES

Our discussion in this book focuses on pluralism in public life — on the kinds of pluralities that are important to contemporary discussions regarding the proper ordering of society. Even here we are aware of being somewhat selective in choosing our pluralisms. It is difficult to think of a plurality that cannot become a subject of heated public debate: people argue about the political significance of theories of creation, methods of contraception, fictional and cinematic portrayals of religious leaders, the relationships between human and nonhuman species, and so on.

We have chosen to highlight three general types of pluralities that are important to public life. Each of these types plays a prominent role in contemporary discussions of the "challenge" of pluralism in public life. We can introduce our typology with an example. Imagine a sociological study that focuses on the Mexican Catholic family. A team of sociologists conducting an extensive investigation of this phenomenon would have to attend to at least three factors. First, they would have to look at familial bonds. The family is a unique pattern of association: it is different from a corporation or a social club. Second, the religious factor would have to be taken into account. Catholic beliefs and practices have a different effect on family life than do Muslim or Hindu ones. A third important consideration is the cultural factor. Mexican families exhibit different patterns than their Armenian or Ethiopian counterparts.

This example illustrates the three types of pluralities that we have in mind as we take on the issues of pluralism in public life. Since we will be making considerable use of these three categories in our discussion, it will help to assign some labels. The religious factor is a case in point for the kind of thing that is commonly referred to as a "philosophy of life" or a "value system." Sometimes when people talk about the need to deal with the increasing pluralism of our contemporary societies, they refer to the diversity of visions of the good life that give direction to people's lives. Such directional visions can be associated with an organized religion or with some other value orientation such as hedonism or Marxism. For lack of a better term, we will consider this type under the label *directional pluralism.*

The family is a mode of human association. It falls on the "natural" end of a spectrum that also includes such associations as highly "voluntary" groups such as clubs and corporations. We will consider this type of plurality as a wrestling with *associational pluralism.*

Our third plurality is made up of differing cultural contexts. We have in mind here the factors Driver lists when he points to those newer movements in theology that draw upon

16

different racial, ethnic, geographic, gender, and class experiences. We label this set of concerns *contextual pluralism*. To be sure, the borders that separate these three categories will not always be easy to discern. But, allowing for some occasional borderline haziness, it is still possible to distinguish three general categories of this sort. A Mexican Catholic family is different from an Italian Catholic family, as well as from a Mexican Pentecostal family and a Mexican Catholic school.

CLASSIFYING PLURALISMS

We have introduced two sets of distinctions. The first set dealt with the ways in which people set forth pluralisms: when they mean to highlight the significance of a specific plurality, they are setting forth a *descriptive* pluralism; when they mean to be advocating a given plurality as a good state of affairs, they are propounding a *normative* pluralism. Our second set of distinctions has to do with three kinds of pluralism that we think are important to public life: the *directional,* the *associational,* and the *contextual.*

It is now necessary in our discussion to observe that these two sets of distinctions can be combined. Each of our three public pluralisms can be set forth as either a descriptive or a normative pluralism. Thus, the examination of various public pluralisms will have to keep these six possibilities in mind:

descriptive directional pluralism:	highlighting the fact of a plurality of directional perspectives
normative directional pluralism:	advocating directional plurality as a good state of affairs
descriptive associational pluralism:	highlighting the fact of a plurality of associational patterns

17

normative associational pluralism:	advocating associational plurality as a good state of affairs
descriptive contextual pluralism:	highlighting the fact of a plurality of cultural contexts
normative contextual pluralism:	advocating contextual plurality as a good state of affairs

Laying the scheme out in this fashion makes it possible for us to indicate the thrust of our argument in this book. We see no difficulties as Christians in endorsing all three descriptive accounts: we have no desire to minimize the significance for contemporary public life of a plurality of directional perspectives, associational patterns, or cultural contexts. On the normative level, we are quite willing to endorse both associational and cultural pluralism. We will set forth some Christian reasons for treating associational and cultural diversity as good states of affairs.

This leaves one kind of pluralism to which we have serious objections: normative directional pluralism. This is the one version of pluralism that would lead us into an ultimate relativism. And since we are convinced that directional relativism is incompatible with a commitment to the gospel, we will be careful to distinguish this version of pluralism from the other manifestations.

CLARIFYING THE ISSUES

We make no pretense that employing the classificatory scheme we have just briefly outlined will "solve" the difficult problems associated with pluralism in public life. But we do hope that we can illuminate at least some of the issues that are at stake in this important and complex area of discussion.

Nor are we motivated by any desire to place pluralism in a bad light. While we have no real sympathy for a thoroughgoing relativistic pluralism, we also are not happy with some of the more simple-minded positions that Christians sometimes set forth as alternatives to relativism. Our evaluations of various attempts to wrestle with pluralism in public life are offered in the hope that we might better understand the genuine challenges that pluralistic phenomena pose, especially — but not only — to the Christian community. We do well, we are convinced, to treat these challenges with the utmost seriousness.

✦ 2 ✦

Thin Consensus, Empty Shrine

IN HIS 1909 Hibbert Lectures, William James told his Oxford audience about the views of a woman whom he described as one of "the philosophic cranks of my acquaintance." Her basic thesis was that reality "is composed of only two elements, the Thick, namely, and the Thin." James observed that this thesis — which, he noted, would probably have brought her some acclaim if she had uttered it in ancient Ionia — has a rather "thin" feel of its own in a modern setting. But, James added, it is still true "as far as it goes."[1]

James's crank might gain some measure of satisfaction from the fact that thickness and thinness continue to receive attention in contemporary philosophy. A noteworthy case in point is the discussion in political thought, triggered by John Rawls's case for a "thin theory of the good," both in his landmark work *A Theory of Justice,* and in his more recent writings.

Rawls's defense of thinness is motivated by his concern to find a just ordering of society in which differing conceptions

---

1. William James, *Essays in Radical Empiricism and a Pluralistic Universe,* vol. 2 (New York: Longmans, Green and Co., 1958), 135-136.

20

of the good life are treated with fairness. How can we deal justly with a diversity of perspectives on the meaning, value, and purpose of human existence? We can only do so, Rawls argues, if we operate with a thin notion of the good. For Rawls this means that we will be able to achieve consensus in the public realm only if we set up our deliberations in such a way that the thick contents[2] of various religious, philosophical, and moral doctrines are not allowed to play a decisive role in public discussions about what is just and fair.

Rawls's arguments are designed to minimize the effects of directional pluralism on the ordering of society. His insistence that thick accounts of human good must not intrude into the discussion of foundational matters pertaining to public life provides a rationale for the widely held conviction that highly textured belief systems — especially those of a religious nature — are "private" matters that ought to have no bearing on the formulation of public policy. His perspective on pluralistic phenomena is an important one for Christians to assess.

"DOMINANT ENDS"

Pluralism does not occur as a technical term in Rawls's *A Theory of Justice*. It is safe to say that this theme was not an explicit item of concern for Rawls when he was writing that

2. Actually, in *A Theory of Justice* (Cambridge, Mass.: Harvard University Press, The Belknap Press, 1971) Rawls typically contrasts "thin" with "full," although in more recent essays he has switched — following the practice of some of his commentators — to "thin" and "thick"; see, for example, Rawls's "Kantian Constructivism in Moral Theory," *Journal of Philosophy* 77, no. 9 (Sept. 1980): 549, where he distinguishes between "a thick and thin veil of ignorance." The "thin/thick" dichotomy as a tool of social analysis has been given currency in recent years by Clifford Geertz (who in turn borrowed it from Gilbert Ryle); see Clifford Geertz, "Thick Description: Toward an Interpretive Theory of Culture," in his *The Interpretation of Cultures* (New York: Basic Books, 1973), 3-30.

book. Indirectly, however, a concern with pluralism is very present in his thinking. This concern is obvious, for example, in his espousal of a societal order in which no "dominant ends" prevail.

Rawls rejects the idea that socio-political life can be held together only by subordination to a single conception of the meaning and purpose of life. Such an arrangement, he is convinced, fails to respect the "heterogeneous" character of human good, and risks promoting fanaticism and intolerance.[3]

Rawls assumes that a genuinely just society would give free rein to a variety of notions about the meaning and purpose of life. Those "intolerant sects" that attempt to impose specific convictions about what it means to serve God upon the society at large are an obvious threat to the maintenance of such a free society.[4]

Rawls has more in mind here than merely the dangers of religious intolerance. He wants to reject all teleological conceptions — all ideas of a dominant end toward which society must aim. The utilitarian conception of the greatest happiness for the greatest number is as suspect in this regard as Ignatius of Loyola's insistence that all of life must be directed to the service of God.[5]

This rejection of a dominant end is crucial for Rawls's understanding of a proper social contract theory. In delineating the basic terms of their association, free and rational persons need only agree on certain general principles for their decision-making. The choice of the ends they will pursue within the societal framework falls outside the terms of the contract; this kind of decision is left to the discretion of the individual parties. What is basic to public decision-making is a set of regulative principles.

3. John Rawls, *A Theory of Justice*, 553-554.
4. Ibid., 215-218.
5. Ibid., 553-560.

As Rawls views things, then, it is not impossible to achieve justice where people hold a plurality of conceptions of the good that human beings ought to pursue. Indeed, Rawls does not seem especially upset by contemporary culture's inability to attain religious or moral consensus. His tone is more positive. Diversity of this sort is a valuable thing. To establish one conception of human good as dominant would stifle our freedom, which includes the liberty to choose the ends toward which we will aim.

Rawls's contracting parties "think of themselves as beings who can and do choose their final ends (always plural in number)"; their aim is "to establish just and favorable conditions for each to fashion his own unity"; they see themselves "as primarily moral persons with an equal right to choose their mode of life."[6] Given the heterogeneity of human selfhood, it is not good for societies or individuals to be subordinate to a single dominant end. Such subordination can only "disfigure" the self.[7]

While these considerations have an obvious bearing on pluralistic thinking, they do not exactly offer us a clear-cut analysis of pluralism. To be sure, when Rawls insists upon the rejection of shared final ends, he is beginning to address the existence of a plurality of notions about the meaning and purpose of life. But he does not move very far into this topic. One reason for this is that Rawls does not pay much attention to the fact of *conflict* among these ends when he discusses them in *A Theory of Justice*. Instead he focuses primarily on the mere diversity of ends; these differing conceptions of meaning and purpose are, as a group, heterogeneous in that they cannot be ranked according to some measure of their intrinsic value. It is only in his later essays that Rawls begins to treat these differing notions of the good as *rival* concep-

6. Ibid., 563.
7. Ibid., 554.

tions, as embodying conflicting accounts of human meaning and purpose.

COOPERATION AND DIVERSITY

In his discussion of dominant ends, Rawls is touching on issues that have to do with what we have labelled directional pluralism. But he also pays some attention in *A Theory of Justice* to matters relating to another of our areas of pluralistic concern: associational pluralism.

Rawls celebrates human diversity with a decidedly aesthetic tone. The "Aristotelian Principle" — according to which, "other things equal, human beings enjoy the exercise of their realized capacities (their innate or trained abilities), and this enjoyment increases the more the capacity is realized, or the greater its complexity"[8] — applies to societies as well as to individuals. People's private lives are but the smallest components in the larger design of society and its public institutions.[9] Each individual is finite, and hence needs other persons, with their special gifts, to help accomplish what he or she could not do alone. Thus Rawls's insistence on the significance of associational diversity:

> It is a feature of human sociability that we are by ourselves but parts of what we might be. We must look to others to attain the excellences that we must leave aside, or lack altogether. The collective activity of society, the many associations and the public life of the largest community that regulates them, sustains our efforts and elicits our contribution.[10]

8. Ibid., 426.
9. Ibid., 528.
10. Ibid., 529.

Rawls is quick to assure us that the social context required for our individual flourishing is not that of a closely knit community that establishes an authoritative common goal that all individuals and associations must pursue ahead of their own interests.[11] Rather, it requires a social order in which public aims are based on principles of justice and this collective activity is perceived as a good. Furthermore, by upholding and maintaining just institutions, individuals and associations best realize their own particular aims and excellences.[12] The principle of cooperation here, Rawls notes, is best understood with a game analogy. Just as a game, when played fairly, manifests a unity of self-interest and common aim, of competitiveness and cooperation, so members of a society can have the common aim of "cooperating together to realize their own and another's nature in ways allowed by the principles of justice."[13]

The brief account Rawls gives in *A Theory of Justice* of the diversity of associations — ranging "from families and friendships to much larger associations" — has a strong voluntarist tone. He never really gives up the position of contracting individuals at his point of departure. Society as such is one great "cooperative venture for mutual advantage," and the smaller associations are also constituted by individuals seeking the mutual advantages of cooperation.[14]

"THE FACT OF PLURALISM"

When we compare Rawls's later essays with the case that he sets forth in *A Theory of Justice,* it is possible to discern a twofold shift in his treatment of the matters we have been discussing. First, he now gives explicit attention to what he

11. Ibid., 528.
12. Ibid., 529.
13. Ibid., 527.
14. Ibid., 520, 527.

calls "the fact of pluralism."[15] And second, he places a strong emphasis on *conflicting* conceptions of the good. Human cooperation now becomes an urgent challenge: how, Rawls asks, is a social unity possible in a society "marked by deep divisions between opposing and incommensurable conceptions of the good"?[16]

What does Rawls mean by "the fact of pluralism"? To begin with, he takes this fact to be "a permanent feature of the public culture of modern democracies."[17] And again, Rawls now characterizes this pluralistic state of affairs in strongly conflictual terms: the fact of pluralism means that any "workable conception of justice" must, in the modern setting,

> allow for a diversity of general and comprehensive doctrines, and for the plurality of conflicting, and indeed incommensurable, conceptions of the meaning, value and purpose of human life (or what I shall call for short "conceptions of the good") affirmed by the citizens of democratic societies.[18]

An obvious next question is what "incommensurable" means as a term for characterizing these diverse conceptions of the good. Here Rawls quickly adopts a stance of metaphysical agnosticism. Unlike the kind of metaphysical pluralism made popular by William James at the beginning of this century, according to which the universe is actually composed of many original principles,[19] Rawls's agnostic

15. John Rawls, "The Idea of an Overlapping Consensus," *Oxford Journal of Legal Studies* 7, no. 1 (Spring 1987): 1.
16. John Rawls, "Justice as Fairness: Political not Metaphysical," *Philosophy and Public Affairs* 14, no. 3 (Summer 1985): 251.
17. Rawls, "Idea of an Overlapping Consensus," 4.
18. Ibid.; Rawls uses similar formulations in his 1985 essay, "Justice as Fairness" — see, e.g., pp. 248-249 — although he does not yet focus directly on "the fact of pluralism" in that essay.
19. See William James, *The Varieties of Religious Experience: A Study*

metaphysics provides us with no judgments about whether or not the conflicts among diverse conceptions of the good extend to the farthest reaches of reality.

Rawls strictly limits the scope of incommensurability to the public domain. For his purposes, he tells us, incommensurability is to be understood as a "political fact"; given the standards available for adjudicating such matters in the public domain, "there is no available political understanding as to how to commensurate these conceptions for settling questions of political justice."[20] It is simply a fact of modern political life, Rawls argues, that there is no longer a consensus regarding the meaning and purpose of human existence. And there is no political test available to us for deciding between better or worse conceptions of the good. Such disputes are about ultimate issues; they have to do with the choices of the ends that we will seek as we give direction to our lives.

In Rawls's scheme, questions of justice can be decided without solving these issues. The deep divisions between opposing and incommensurable conceptions of the good do not rule out the possibility of public consensus. Such is indeed the message of Rawls's later essays. The theme is a hopeful one: consensus is not out of reach; social unity is still possible, for citizens can publicly agree on a "political conception of *justice*" as a basis for the social order. Rawls believes that justice is a concept "independent from and prior to" goodness, because it sets limits on the concepts of goodness that a society will permit.[21]

Yet while Rawls advocates the separation of justice and the good — the shielding off of the public domain from substantive ethical, metaphysical, religious matters — he is

---

in Human Nature, Gifford Lectures on natural religion delivered at Edinburgh in 1901-1902 (New York: Random House, The Modern Library, 1939), see Lecture VI.

20. Rawls, "Idea of an Overlapping Consensus," 4n.6.
21. Rawls, "Justice as Fairness," 249.

careful not to denigrate these more particular perspectives. His idea of an "overlapping consensus" is meant to bring about a separation while avoiding an attitude of indifference toward conceptions of the good. Let us briefly examine his attempt to accomplish this feat.

THE PROPRIETY OF SEPARATION

Rawls doesn't advocate a complete severance of ethical questions from political deliberations about justice. He sees *some* connection between the good and the right. An attempt at complete separation would obviously lead to some absurdities: it would mean, for example, that people would be asked to adopt principles of justice, and to spell out an agreement about rights and liberties and opportunities, without being able to say that all of these matters are *good* things to strive for. This clearly is not Rawls's position. His account of the relationship between the right and the good is a rather subtle one. We will not attempt therefore to chart out all of its complexities here; instead we will focus on the issues that have an obvious bearing on the topic of pluralism.

Granting, then, that Rawls does not mean to attempt a complete severance, how is it that he can accept some sort of — even minimal — connection between the good and the right while still maintaining that the principles of justice are not to be influenced by specific visions of the good? Rawls's answer here relies on his distinction between thick and thin accounts of the good. The basic thrust of his position is set forth clearly in *A Theory of Justice:* a workable theory of justice requires only a thin account of the good. Such a thin account would be noncontroversial; it would itself be an abstraction from thicker conceptions of the good.

Rawls requires this process of abstraction to produce a thin account of the good that avoids significant metaphysical entanglements. The seriousness of this requirement is under-scored by his refusal to associate his own efforts to establish a liberal theory with the liberal programs of Kant and Mill. The Kantian and Millian conceptions, Rawls complains, are metaphysically rooted in presuppositions regarding the iden-tity of the self. They propagate a specific philosophical view of human nature, and their doctrines of free institutions are based on values which are held by few members of democratic societies. They take too much for granted. Thus the liberalism of Kant and Mill is really only "another sectarian doctrine."[22] Rawls's search, then, is for a liberal theory without metaphysical roots, drawing only on "certain funda-mental intuitive ideas" implicit in "the public culture of a democratic society."[23] It does not even need, he thinks, a philosophical anthropology — a point stressed by Rorty in a lengthy essay celebrating the themes of Rawls's recent pub-lications. Rawls's account relies on no philosophical premises at all, Rorty insists; it appeals only to "history and soci-ology."[24]

Rawls himself prefers a slightly more nuanced portrayal of his project. He admits that there is in fact a "normative" or "moral" view of the person implied in his theory.[25] But this notion of personhood is not very complicated. In contrast to a detailed theory of human nature, it is merely the sort of understanding of proper personhood that fits a society's sense of the "general facts about human nature and society."[26]

22. Ibid., 245-247.
23. Ibid., 236n.19.
24. Richard Rorty, "The Priority of Democracy to Philosophy," in *The Virginia Statute for Religious Freedom: Its Evolution and Consequences in American History,* ed. Merrill D. Peterson and Robert C. Vaughan (New York: Cambridge University Press, 1988), 262.
25. Rawls, "Justice as Fairness," 232n.15.
26. Rawls, "Kantian Constructivism," 534.

INDIFFERENCE OR AVOIDANCE?

Again, Rawls's insistence that the good can be separated from the right is not without its subtleties. Nonetheless, he does think that in a significant sense we can achieve the kind of just ordering of society that will be agreeable to people who operate with very different understandings of what makes for human flourishing.

Rawls's underlying assumption here seems to be that this sort of theoretical separation is possible because when it comes to our actual practice in the public realm, we find that there is indeed no need to connect our specific moral and metaphysical beliefs with our conceptions of public justice. Citizens may view their own ultimate ends very differently, Rawls observes, from the way they view the norms they abide by in the public arena. This difference can even be thought of in terms of different "identities" that we possess as individuals, one "public" and the other "non-public." Someone's private self can experience a pervasive change — along the Damascus road "Saul of Tarsus becomes Paul the Apostle" — without a corresponding transformation in public selfhood.[27]

Rawls, however, is not expressing indifference or skepticism toward metaphysical conceptions of the good life. Richard Rorty seems seriously to misunderstand Rawls's intentions in this regard. Having cited Thomas Jefferson's comment that "it does me no injury for my neighbor to say that there are twenty Gods or no God," he goes on to link Jefferson and Rawls in a common commitment to grounding public indifference to religious matters on skeptical foundations. Rorty defends both thinkers against the charge that they themselves presuppose metaphysical conceptions:

27. Rawls, "Justice as Fairness," 241-242.

Both Jefferson and Rawls would have to reply, "I have no arguments for my dubious theological-metaphysical claim, because I do not know how to discuss such issues, and do not want to. My interest is in helping to preserve and create political institutions that will foster public indifference to such issues, while putting no restrictions on private discussion of them."[28]

To attribute a basic indifference about such issues to Rawls is to misread his intentions. In *A Theory of Justice* he explicitly rejects skepticism about or indifference toward metaphysical and religious questions.[29] And in the later essays, propounding what he calls "the method of avoidance," he is eager to dissociate himself from the view that "these questions are unimportant or regarded with indifference."[30]

This is no minor quibble over terminology. What is at stake is nothing less than the status of "the fact of pluralism." As we have seen, Rawls has come to define pluralism in terms of conflicting conceptions of ultimate ends. Promoting indifference to these matters would be advocating indifference to pluralism itself — pluralism would cease to function as a fact of public experience. Indeed, it would be odd for Rawls, having insisted that "the fact of pluralism" is a significant feature of modern democratic society, to treat the existence of conflicting conceptions of the good as a matter of complete indifference in discussions of public justice!

Rawls manifests his intentions in his idea of an overlapping consensus. The core contention here is that while people come into the public domain from very different metaphysical/religious/moral starting points, once they have arrived they can agree to operate with the same intuitive ideas about

28. Rorty, "Priority of Democracy," 276n.15.
29. Rawls, *A Theory of Justice,* 214, 243.
30. Rawls, "Justice as Fairness," 230; see also Rawls, "Idea of an Overlapping Consensus," 8, 12-13, 20.

what goes into a just arrangement. They can reach a consensus on such matters as the rule of law, liberty of conscience, freedom of thought, equality of opportunity, a fair share of material means for all citizens — notwithstanding the divergent conceptions and motivations on the basis of which they defend those conditions for justice. Rawls holds out the hope that their "different premises may lead to the same conclusions" in the public arena.[31]

Rawls imagines a case where citizens embrace the same principles of public justice but for very different reasons. One group affirms the principles because of its religious outlook, another group as a consequence of a Kantian-type liberal doctrine, while a third group embraces the same principles simply for their own sake, without interest in extra-political support and justification. Not only does Rawls contend that a consensus of this sort is feasible, but, interestingly enough, he even claims that the resultant unity would be "far more stable" than one obtained on the basis of skepticism, indifference, or a prudent *modus vivendi*.[32]

Rawls does not advocate indifference. His "method of avoidance" is not meant to guarantee that questions of public life be debated in a metaphysical/religious/moral vacuum; rather, it is a means of preventing any one of those conceptions from being the primary shaper of the policies resulting from such deliberation. Indeed, Rawls is convinced that his thin theory of the good can only be arrived at by a "thinning-out" of the conflicting thicknesses that are a real presence in modern political life. Still, this deals with Rawls's actual intentions. It is also important to ask whether his theory can actually accomplish what he intends. It is not clear that it can.

31. Rawls, "Idea of an Overlapping Consensus," 9.
32. Rawls, "Justice as Fairness," 250; see also Rawls, "Idea of an Overlapping Consensus," 9-10, 18-19.

For one thing, even though his idea of an overlapping consensus does show that "the fact of pluralism" is not just an extra-political reality, it is still the case that the pluralism of ends has no intrinsic connection to the public realm in his scheme. The relationship is extrinsic and contingent.

While Rawls does hold that conflicting conceptions of ultimate ends are at work in modern life, he professes — as we have seen — an agnostic position regarding the nature of those differences. Nowhere, for example, does he tell us *why* he thinks that the apparently different conceptions of the good are in reality incommensurable.

Even though Rorty has misconstrued Rawls's actual intentions, the Rawlsian scheme is indeed vulnerable to Rorty's attribution of skepticism. Rawls's "fact of pluralism" presupposes that incommensurable differences regarding the nature of the good constitute a significant feature of modern democratic life. But he offers no arguments for his claim that irresolvable metaphysical/moral/religious differences are crucial to the democratic experience. Certain conceptions of the good happen to be "available" to us in our attempts "to constitute an overlapping consensus," and some of them are likely to persevere and even thrive in a society that allows diverse viewpoints to interact within a just framework.[33]

Not only is the said relation between the plurality of conceptions of the good and modern political society a contingent one; once the overlapping consensus has been reached, for Rawls, there is little further use for those thick conceptions which made the thinning-out process necessary in the first place. Apparently Rawls would not count it as a loss if all thick conceptions would disappear — although, in fact, he does judge it "likely" that they will continue to thrive. Nor do they seem to gain any strength for their survival from

33. Ibid., 226, 250, and Rawls, "Idea of an Overlapping Consensus," 5, 9.

the concept of public justice to which they have lent their support.

Once again Rorty probes a vulnerable point in Rawls's account. He notes that Rawls does in fact suggest that not all conceptions of the good will thrive, but some will die off. Rorty then draws this parallel:

> The suggestion that there are many philosophical views that will *not* survive in such conditions is analogous to the Enlightenment suggestion that the adoption of democratic institutions will cause "superstitious" forms of religious belief gradually to die off.[34]

Whether Rawls means to promote such an attitude toward specific conceptions of the good is, of course, debatable. And whether his theory actually promotes this perspective, quite apart from his conscious intentions, is also a matter that can only be decided by a much more detailed analysis — and by further clarification from Rawls as to how his agnosticism is to be distinguished from a thoroughgoing skepticism.

PRESERVING PARTICULARITIES

Whatever concerns Christians may have about the details of Rawls's theory, there is no excuse for ignoring the important positive challenge that his project poses for Christian thought. The question of how justice is possible in a society characterized by diverse religious, moral, and philosophical beliefs is an important one for Christians to clarify.

Harlan Beckley has responded to the challenge of the Rawlsian project by providing it with a strong and thoughtful

---

34. Rorty, "Priority of Democracy," 275n.8.

Christian defense.[35] Beckley insists that Rawls's account of justice can be properly construed as allowing for the existence of "a distinctively Christian ethic alongside a common conception of justice."[36] Beckley himself insists upon an important role for a uniquely Christian ethical perspective. Since many of the moral issues that Christians face have nothing to do with distributive justice or the need to recognize the rights of others, believers will often appeal to distinctively Christian considerations in deciding how to act.[37] But Beckley is also convinced that if the constraint of publicness is to be realized, Christians must find a way of bracketing their distinctive beliefs when thinking about some of the basic issues of public order.[38] Given the plurality of conflicting aims at work in modern society,

> we cannot arrive at common principles merely by purging our selfish interests or by moral reasoning among rational persons who insist upon basing justice on their full conceptions of the good. The only possibility for moral agreement (short of all persons converting to a single perspective) is to abstract from differing particular conceptions of the good and morality. This process of abstraction is an attempt to discover general beliefs, ends, and principles which persons with diverse particular beliefs and values can embrace.[39]

Contrasting his own interpretation of Rawls with that of Jeffrey Stout, who sees "Rawls as abstracting from religious

35. Harlan R. Beckley, "A Christian Affirmation of Rawls's Idea of Justice as Fairness: Part I," *Journal of Religious Ethics* 13, no. 2 (Fall 1985): 210-242, and "A Christian Affirmation . . . : Part II," *Journal of Religious Ethics* 14, no. 2 (Fall 1986): 229-246.
36. Beckley, "Christian Affirmation . . . : Part I," 214.
37. Ibid.
38. Ibid., 216.
39. Ibid., 222.

beliefs in order to establish an eternal perspective which 'displaces' the beliefs of historical religious communities," Beckley insists that Rawls is not trying to eliminate particular conceptions of the good. Rather, Rawls's point is to abstract from particular conceptions of the good that are present in a specific set of historical circumstances, a general principle that would be fair to, but would not override, all those diverse perspectives.[40]

Beckley sees no insurmountable problems that would keep Christians from accepting the thin account of the good in the Rawlsian scheme. To accept this account is not to surrender peculiarly Christian convictions. Such a surrendering is precisely what Rawls's overlapping consensus is designed to prevent:

> According to this interpretation, affirming the idea of justice as fairness does not require that Christians give up or relegate to irrelevancy their distinctive beliefs and conceptions of the good in order to agree to a universal conception of justice. It invites Christians to consider whether their distinctive beliefs and values embrace, for purposes of addressing the subject of justice only, Rawls's more general beliefs that persons are free, rational, and equal.[41]

RAWLSIAN ABSTRACTION

Beckley's assessment does not set to rest questions about the compatibility of the Rawlsian project with Christian beliefs. Is Beckley correct, for example, in his assumption that Rawls's program of abstracting general principles from diverse religious belief systems is a workable one? Rawls and Beckley

40. Ibid., 223-224; Beckley's reference is to Jeffrey ·Stout, *The Flight from Authority* (Notre Dame, Ind.: University of Notre Dame Press, 1981), 235.
41. Ibid., 237.

are both optimistic about the possibility of a common conception of justice not biased in favor of a specific conception of the good. But Rawls's critics have regularly expressed the concern that he is in fact espousing a particular view of human flourishing, namely that of the liberal perspective. Liberal conceptions seem to be at work, for example, in Rawls's basic notions about what sort of irresolvable dispute can be set aside in deliberating about questions of justice. As Richard Fern has observed, Rawls wants to describe "the original position" in a manner that will "avoid philosophical contention." But the very "assumption that there is no ascertainable truth as regards the good or, more narrowly, the existence of God" is quite a matter of contention! "[W]here else," asks Fern, "is there so deep and unresolved a problem?"[42] Similarly, Michael Sandel has argued that Rawls's emphasis on toleration is dependent upon the liberal conviction that the state should give citizens freedom to choose their own values, imposing as little as possible in this regard.[43]

Again, legitimate questions can be raised here about the degree to which Rawlsian abstraction succeeds in generating an account of justice that is free from assumptions rooted in a specific conception of the good. But we can also legitimately ask whether Rawls has made a convincing case that abstraction is itself necessary in order to provide a foundation for public justice.

For example, when Beckley argues for the compatibility of Rawls's notion of abstraction with Christian beliefs, he does so by arguing against those Christian thinkers who insist that Christians have no business looking for "common principles of morality" that can be agreed upon by believers and nonbelievers alike. Stanley Hauerwas's position is a case in

42. Richard Fern, "Religious Belief in a Rawlsian Society," *Journal of Religious Ethics* 15, no. 1 (Spring 1987): 45.
43. Michael J. Sandel, "The Political Theory of the Procedural Republic," *Revue de métaphysique et de morale* 93, no. 1 (1988): 57.

point here: by concentrating too much on distributive justice, Hauerwas contends, Christians run the risk of bartering away their distinctive message regarding political questions.[44]

Yet we need to ask whether the only alternative to Rawlsian abstraction is a "thick" pessimism about the possibility of achieving any sort of general agreement on principles of justice. Might it not be possible to agree with Rawls that public life does require the constraint of publicness, while disagreeing with his insistence that this constraint can be arrived at only by abstracting the thin universal from thick particularities?

In our first chapter we mentioned John Murray Cuddihy's argument that Christian civility can be based upon a specific understanding of Christian eschatological teachings. Though we will examine this important suggestion in more detail further on, it is worth mentioning at this point as a way of grounding the constraint of publicness that doesn't fit the Rawlsian scheme. Rawls thinks that political civility can only be cultivated by releasing ourselves from the pull of particularistic convictions as we step into the public arena. The constraint of publicness can only occur when we employ abstraction as a means of moving away from specific conceptions of the good. Cuddihy, on the other hand, is suggesting something very different: that a specific vision like that of Christian belief provides us with resources for nurturing an inner constraint of publicness — one that draws on the very thickness that Rawls wants to thin out! Cuddihy's suggestion is worth exploring, and we will return to it as our discussion proceeds. The kind of inner constraint that he proposes is, we think, the only sort of resource that can give adequate grounding to the constraint of publicness.

One general advantage of Cuddihy's proposal is that it

---

44. Stanley Hauerwas, *A Community of Character* (Notre Dame, Ind.: University of Notre Dame Press, 1981), 3; for Beckley's reference to Hauerwas's view, see "Christian Affirmation . . . . : Part I," 224.

stems from a deep desire to preserve particularities in the process of promoting public civility. Even if Rawlsian abstraction does succeed as a method, it appears to destroy those particulars that serve as its point of departure. This is the problem with Beckley's much-repeated insistence that Rawlsian abstraction does not mean displacement. The process of abstracting as Rawls understands it seems to draw on a universalizing tendency inimical to the production and maintenance of conflicting particularities.

Basil Mitchell has offered an interesting argument that is relevant to this point. He contends that thinkers who rely heavily on universalizing programs lack "a sense of depth and the uniqueness of the individual." Their efforts to find a moral perspective that will satisfy diverse human aims and purposes are bound to fail, since they operate with too meager a moral base. It is precisely because of this, Mitchell argues, that romanticist impulses come into play. Romantics protest against a thin moral consensus by featuring the very kinds of factors that universalizers cannot adequately account for: the passions, the imagination, the urge to personal commitment. But, says Mitchell, romanticism also fails because it, too, is incapable of sustaining a stable culture. Small doses of romanticism can fertilize the cultural soil, but large doses rob the soil of its nurturing power. Neither the thin universalizers nor the thick romanticists, then, can provide what is necessary for a healthy culture.[45]

THE "EMPTY SHRINE"

It is one thing to insist that we must find an alternative to both thin universalizing and thick romanticizing, but it is another

---

45. Basil Mitchell, *Morality: Religious and Secular: The Dilemma of the Traditional Conscience* (Oxford: Oxford University Press, Clarendon Press, 1980), 46.

thing to find the alternative. There are certainly Christian thinkers who would insist at this point that, given the record of failed efforts at finding a third way between these two options, we should not give up too quickly on the universalizing program.

Michael Novak's efforts to defend a thin conception of the good are worth considering in this regard. While Novak's writings show no signs of serious interaction with Rawls's thinking, he shares Rawls's conviction that specific conceptions of the good should not shape public policy. Since Novak harnesses this conviction to the cause of Roman Catholic social thought, it will be interesting to devote some attention to Novak's efforts — especially in *The Spirit of Democratic Capitalism* (1983) and *Freedom with Justice* (1984) — if only to be sure that our nervousness about the separation of particularistic thickness from public discourse is not especially linked to the peculiarities of Rawls's more secularist formulations.

Interestingly, in one of the few places where Novak mentions Rawls, he emphasizes his differences with Rawls. Novak thinks that Rawls starts with the individual, giving only secondary consideration to social arrangements, whereas Novak wants to take as his point of departure the individual who is from the beginning to be found "*within* lived social worlds."[46] This way of describing their differences is somewhat misleading, of course, given Rawls's strong emphasis on "cooperation." But it is also slightly misleading as a way of depicting Novak's own position. He actually gives more positive attention to the idea of a free individual than this brief characterization suggests. Indeed, the competitive individual figures prominently in Novak's basic account of the nature of societal pluralism. And the fact of pluralism is very much on Novak's mind as he develops his perspective.

---

46. Michael Novak, *The Spirit of Democratic Capitalism* (New York: Simon and Schuster, A Touchstone Book, 1983), 61.

Novak distinguishes his "democratic capitalism" from two other societal patterns: those associated with traditionalist and socialist type schemes. Each of these types produces a closed society whose "unitary order" is held together by a collective vision of the good and the true. Sooner or later, Novak thinks, a unitary moral order will give rise to "a unitary political power" that will seek to impose its concept of the good on all citizens. Novak rejects these unitary schemes in favor of a free, pluralistic society wherein public virtues depend only upon the cooperation of free individuals.[47] Here there is no unitarian order, no single code, and hence no attempt to impose a specific moral-cultural vision on the political and socio-economic realms.

It is in this context that Novak introduces the metaphor of the "empty shrine." Instead of a "socially imposed vision of the good," capitalist democracy displays a "reverential emptiness at the heart of pluralism."[48] It must be quickly added that Novak connects this emptiness with a respect for "transcendence" and not with an indifferent or skeptical attitude regarding matters of ultimate concern. The reverential emptiness that he has in mind occurs when a society, in a deliberate act of self-limitation, refrains from attempts to define and codify the meaning and purpose of human life.[49] Indeed, it is probably out of a desire to highlight a sense of respect for the transcendent that Novak employs religiously laden expressions — "reverential," "shrine" — in describing the emptiness:

In a genuinely pluralistic society, there is no one sacred canopy. *By intention* there is not. At its spiritual core, there is an empty shrine. That shrine is left empty in the knowl-

47. Ibid., 49, 60, 69.
48. Ibid., 68.
49. Ibid., 55.

edge that no one word, image, or symbol is worthy of what all seek there. Its emptiness, therefore, represents the transcendence which is approached by free consciences from a virtually infinite number of directions.[50]

Note that the "pluralistic" state of affairs here has to do with a plurality of visions of the good. While this places Novak close to Rawls, there is one important difference between them: Novak does not embrace a Rawlsian agnosticism about conceptions of the good. While Rawls refrained from all claims to the truth-value of ultimate ends, Novak is ready to grant that these various visions point to true transcendence. Indeed, their very plurality has to do with the fact that transcendence can be approached "from a virtually infinite number of directions."

Novak is dealing here with directional pluralism. But he is also very interested in a kind of associational pluralism. Society has come to be differentiated, he argues, into three semi-autonomous systems: the political, the economic, and the moral-cultural.[51] This development is, says Novak, a welcome achievement of modern life. Traditional societies are characterized by a solidarism that leaves no room for differentiation — a pattern that can reappear under modern conditions:

> When capitalism reverts to state control (as it did under fascism and does under forms of socialist collectivism), it ceases to be capitalism and becomes once again the patrimonial state. Differentiation between the economic system and the political system is then swallowed up again in primeval unity. The state rules all.[52]

50. Ibid., 53.
51. Ibid., 45-48, 56, 171-186; in employing this three-part distinction, Novak acknowledges the influence of Daniel Bell's *The Cultural Contradictions of Capitalism* (New York: Basic Books, 1976).
52. Ibid., 46.

Only a rich associational diversity can provide a proper antidote to statism. Novak quotes at length the well-known passage where de Tocqueville refers glowingly to "the immense assemblage of associations" present in the United States. This passage concludes with de Tocqueville's graphic advocacy of the formation of associations as a counterpoise to the egalitarian tendencies of democracy: "If men are to remain civilized, or to become so, the art of associating together must grow and improve, in the same ratio in which the equality of conditions is increased."[53]

De Tocqueville's comments nicely illustrate Novak's concerns. We can see, for example, why Novak is uneasy with what he sees as Rawls's emphasis on the contracting individual. And in spite of the fact that Novak is not being quite fair to Rawls on this score, Novak's emphasis on the communitarian individual, along with his insistence on the importance of "mediating structures,"[54] suggests that his treatment of pluralism will be more nuanced than Rawls's.

Unfortunately Novak's actual discussion fails to deliver on this promise. While he begins with a notion of the difference between directional and associational pluralism, for the most part he runs the two together. As a consequence, "unitary order" may denote at one and the same time a society guided by a single ethico-religious vision, as well as one without differentiation of the political, economic, and moral-cultural spheres. Similarly Novak uses "pluralist order" to refer indiscriminately both to competing visions of the good and to a differentiated society in which the three spheres mentioned above retain a measure of relative autonomy.

53. Alexis de Tocqueville, *Democracy in America,* trans. Henry Reeve, ed. Phillips Bradley, 2 vols. (New York: Vintage Books, 1945), vol. 2, 118, quoted in Michael Novak, *Freedom with Justice: Catholic Social Thought and Liberal Institutions* (San Francisco: Harper and Row, 1984), 195.
54. Novak, *Freedom with Justice,* 162, 201-208.

Of course, in many historical situations the directional and the associational do coincide. Often a unitary society in the one sense is also unitarian in the other, just as associational differentiation often goes hand in hand with directional pluralism. But to show that the connections here are necessary ones takes more argument than Novak provides.

CHRISTIAN EMPTINESS?

How can Novak advocate that the central shrine in the public place be left empty while claiming to promote the cause of Christian thought? Or more pointedly: how does he mean to reconcile, in the words of the subtitle of his *Freedom with Justice*, "Catholic Social Thought and Liberal Institutions"?

His professed commitment to "liberal institutions" is crucial in this regard. Nowhere does Novak make a case for uniquely Catholic modes of association. We find no pleading in his writings on behalf of Catholic labor unions, Catholic parties, or even Catholic educational institutions. His clear preference is for associations that are based on a consensus that is not dependent on any one particular religion.[55] Nevertheless, the Catholic contribution is, for Novak, inspirational. It helps to build a public ethos, rather than providing specific (non-ecclesiastical) institutions.

This is, of course, a somewhat limited version of the scope of "Catholic social thought." But even on this more limited account, Novak offers only a guarded endorsement. Novak does not think, for example, that democratic capitalism is totally dependent on Roman Catholic, or even more broadly Christian, inspiration for its sustenance. He assumes

55. See Novak's "Religion and Liberty: From Vision to Politics," *Christian Century* 105, no. 21 (July 6-13, 1988): 635-638.

that the principle of cooperation was already firmly established in the theory and practice of 19th-century liberalism,[56] so that it was the function of the associative ethos of Christianity and Judaism to reinforce what had already been established as indispensable.[57] Liberalism, then, doesn't merely supply us with the institutions, it also contributes some of the inspiration, by doing its own part to shape the requisite ethos and virtues.

Novak is explicit in his rejection of some of the elements contained in Catholic social thought. Specifically, he castigates the way Roman Catholic teachings have been used to support both conservative solidarism, which takes its cue from the unitary order of traditional societies, and socialism, which he views as an anachronistic attempt to impose a unitary order on pluralistic modernity. He finds the church's social encyclicals wanting in many respects — much evidence on this point is found in part II of *Freedom and Justice*. And not even papal teachings escape his critique; Pius II, for example, is chided for his "flirtation with Marxist analysis and his disdain for the ideology of liberalism."[58]

THE RELEVANCE OF CHRISTIAN THOUGHT

What then is Novak's positive message as a Christian? Surely there is more to it than a defense of the emptiness of the "central shrine" in a world threatened by solidarism and socialism. Is it the prime function of Catholic social thought, when purified of solidarist and socialist elements, to help liberalism guard the "reverential emptiness at the heart of pluralism"?

56. See, e.g., Novak, *Freedom with Justice*, 78, 117.
57. Ibid., 198.
58. Ibid., 147.

Novak does grant a greater role to Catholic social thought than that of merely assisting liberalism. To be sure, he insists that Christian "symbols" — whatever their importance in other respects — ought not to have a place at the center of a pluralist society. But Novak clearly wants to prevent separation from sliding into skeptical indifference — a genuine danger, as we have seen, in Rawls's thought. Rather, Novak attempts to provide a Christian grounding for the espousal of pluralism:

> Christian symbols ought not to be placed in the center of a pluralist society. They must not be, out of reverence for the transcendent which others approach in other ways. Yet . . . the underlying philosophy of pluralism is consonant with Jewish and Christian understandings of human life.[59]

Novak's notion of consonance is meant to preserve a distinction between two orders. Religion views the human condition *sub specie aeternitatis:* it deals with our creatureliness, our proneness to corruption, our sociability, etc. Pluralism pertains to the historical order of modern society. The two ways of ordering our experience remain distinct. But while liberalism is seen as the most adequate socio-economic and political body of doctrines with respect to the second order, Novak does want religious ideas to have some influence on the way pluralism is structured. A genuinely pluralist society "reflects the image of the Blessed Trinity, the Creator of all things, Lord of history, Spirit brooding over dark creation."[60] In Novak's understanding of the consonance relationship, religious ideas have their own integrity, and the test of a healthy pluralism will have to do with the ways in which the pluralistic order "reflects" the religious order. Yet

59. Ibid., 70.
60. Ibid., 164.

Catholicism plays another role that goes beyond offering a mere inspirational assist to pluralism: religion also serves as a *restraining* influence on public life.

Novak does not equate the endorsement of pluralism with the espousal of relativism:

> It simply is not true that all right-thinking persons, in all conscience and with all goodwill, hold the same vision of the good and judge moral acts similarly. Pluralism in moral vision is real. To recognize this is not to surrender to moral relativism. It does not follow from the fact that persons (and groups) stand in radical moral disagreement that "anything goes," "to each his own," etc. It may well be that when persons or groups stand in radical moral disagreement, only one is correct. The problem for a free society is to discern which.[61]

Novak makes it clear that the network of liberal institutions will not by itself generate the criteria for deciding which of the competing visions is the correct one. In fact, it may be very important for a society, in a given situation, to decide in favor of one or another of these competing visions. What is to be done in such a situation? Novak does not develop his answer in very explicit terms. He is, however, clear on at least these two items. One is his strong opposition to the use of moral coercion. And the second is his confidence in the restraining power of the moral ideals that are exhibited in the Jewish and Christian traditions.

This is an improvement on Rawls's position, not only because it pays closer attention to the positive role of Christian conviction in public life, but also because it takes seriously the ways in which religious ideals can nurture spiritual resources for the requisite restraint. We have already ad-

61. Novak, *Spirit of Democratic Capitalism,* 63.

dressed the importance of "inner" dimensions in the constraint of publicness. But we must ask whether it is misguided to think that religious ideals can do the job in the pluralistic setting Novak intends for them. We will pursue this question in the next chapter by examining the views of some contemporary thinkers who insist that the constraint of publicness can only be guaranteed by a societal arrangement in which the public shrine is not quite as empty as Rawls and Novak want it to be.

Religion and the Public Square

JOHN RAWLS wants the principles of justice to be established in such a way that they are not dependent upon specific ethical, religious, or metaphysical perspectives. And Michael Novak attempts to articulate a Christian theory that, while much less ambitious than Rawls's account, aims at the maintenance of a public space that has been cleared of any unitary vision of the good life.

Do these projects succeed? *Can* they succeed? We have already expressed some doubts about whether Rawls and Novak can in fact deliver on what they promise. We must now address this matter in more detail. We will explore the possibility that these kinds of thinning/emptying projects are themselves dependent upon particular views about historical development and the proper patterns of human flourishing. More specifically, we will consider the possibility that these projects take for granted the secularist thesis that public life has become, or will soon become, entirely *post*-religious — the implication being that henceforth religion's only relevance is restricted to the private domain.

We will pursue this line of argument by considering the views of Richard Neuhaus and Lesslie Newbigin. These two writers have argued at length that the attempt to create an empty public shrine is itself anything but neutral.

IMPOSSIBLE NAKEDNESS

In his much discussed book *The Naked Public Square* and in other writings, Richard Neuhaus offers a sustained critique of all those who want to remove religious influences from public life. But he also sees more at work in these attempts at "nakedness" than a mere focus on the role — or the absence — of organized religion in discussions of public policy. The anti-religionists often exhibit a "hostility to normative culture" as such.[1]

Rawls receives special criticism in this regard; Rawls's hoped-for "exclusion of religion from the public arena is part of the exclusion of the culturally normative." The result of the Rawlsian project, argues Neuhaus, is the creation of public persons who are nothing more than "anonymous, deracinated, dehistoricized rational beings defining justice behind a 'veil of ignorance.'" And while Rawls's strictures against normative issues are defended in the name of pluralism, they result in a sterile monism. Protecting the peaceful coexistence of a plurality of life-styles and values against the divisive effects of debates about normative issues actually leads to the very opposite of a genuine pluralism: a mere juxtaposition of ideas bereft of their truth-claims, a deliberate indifference to the ideals and values that people actually profess.[2]

In this context we can understand Neuhaus's striking characterization of pluralism as "a jealous god." For wherever "pluralism is established as dogma," he argues, "there is no

1. Richard John Neuhaus, "From Providence to Privacy: Religion and the Redefinition of America," in *Unsecular America*, ed. Richard J. Neuhaus (Grand Rapids, Mich.: Wm. B. Eerdmans Publ. Co., 1986), 66.

2. Ibid., 56, 61, 63.

room for other dogmas. The assertion of other points of reference in moral discourse becomes, by definition, a violation of pluralism."[3]

What Rawls and other "radical relativizers" fail to recognize is that religion can never be successfully reduced to a private concern. Since religion has to do with our relationship to the ultimate meaning and value found in every aspect of human existence, and since public life is ineluctably drawn to matters of ultimate concern, religion is bound to reassert itself in the public sphere:

> religion and politics contend for dominance over the same territory. Both are political in the sense of being engaged in a struggle for power. Both are religious in the sense of making a total claim upon life.[4]

On Neuhaus's view, nakedness cannot be a lasting situation. Or, to use Novak's image, the public shrine cannot long be left empty. Public life is characterized by a *horror vacui:* public emptiness "is at best a transitional phenomenon. It is a vacuum begging to be filled."[5]

This much is clear. But what is Neuhaus telling us about the relationship between religion and politics as such? Is politics inherently religious, in that it inevitably strives for ultimacy, always refusing to stay within its proper bounds? Or does it nurture a religious type of impulse only once it begins to dominate public life in its entirety? Because Neuhaus does not address these important questions, he fails to provide an adequate or systematic account of the role of religion in public life.

3. Richard J. Neuhaus, *The Naked Public Square: Religion and Democracy in America* (Grand Rapids, Mich.: Wm. B. Eerdmans Publ. Co., 1984), 148.
4. Ibid.
5. Ibid., 86.

PUBLIC AND PRIVATE

The basic arguments of Lesslie Newbigin's *Foolishness to the Greeks* show some close parallels to the case set forth by Neuhaus, even though the two thinkers write from rather different contexts. *The Naked Public Square* addresses issues that loom large in North American debates about civil religion and the separation of church and state. Bishop Newbigin's discussion, on the other hand, bears the marks of the shock that he experienced when, upon returning to his native England after serving for forty years as a missionary in India, he found a public mood at work that was more inimical to the gospel than the spiritual climate of Indian society. Perhaps this explains why Newbigin is more interested than Neuhaus is in constructing a systematic account of the spread of secularism.

Newbigin's focus is the dichotomy between the public and the private realms. He sees the Enlightenment's strong separation between value and fact as the single most important cause of the public/private rift. Values were relegated to the private realm while facts were given the privilege of public status. This worldview, according to Newbigin, evolved into the mainstay of secularism: religion was reduced to a matter of "values" and was thereby relegated to the sphere of private concerns.[6]

The Enlightenment outlook also eliminates the notion of purpose from the realm of proper scientific understanding.[7] When nonteleological explanations are accepted as the standard for public life, neutrality regarding values and ultimate ends comes to have the status of a dogma.

Nevertheless Enlightenment thinkers could not destroy what Newbigin sees as the inherent purposiveness of human nature; hence the quest for "neutrality" itself became a pur-

---

6. Lesslie Newbigin, *Foolishness to the Greeks* (Grand Rapids, Mich.: Wm. B. Eerdmans Publ. Co., 1986), 35-37, 40.
7. Ibid., 24.

posive endeavor, evolving into a project pursued with religious zeal. Because these spiritual currents are at work in public life, Newbigin — like Neuhaus — is convinced that Novak's hope for an empty shrine is misguided: "The shrine does not remain empty. If the one true image, Jesus Christ, is not there, an idol will take its place."[8]

RELIGION AS CRITIQUE

Thus far there is a formal agreement between Newbigin's and Neuhaus's accounts, though the former gives a more systematic treatment to the secularist outlook. But they do disagree on a matter that is important to our discussion: while Neuhaus holds out for a popular public consensus, Newbigin offers a rather straightforward endorsement of public pluralism. His pluralistic sympathies are clearly exhibited in his critique of the perspective that Peter Berger defends in his *The Heretical Imperative,* where Berger continues his long-standing argument that pluralism is the salient feature of modernity.

According to Berger the present-day pluralist situation is a result of the disappearance of the traditional kind of "plausibility structure" that defines accepted patterns of belief — and which to depart from is to engage in "heresy," a term that comes from *hairesis*, meaning choosing for oneself. We moderns are all confronted, says Berger, with the "necessity of choosing between gods" — thus "the heretical imperative."[9]

Newbigin agrees with this characterization of modernity. But he disagrees with Berger's account of how we are to go about choosing our gods. Since Berger does not want to relegate religion to the private-subjective sphere, he insists

8. Ibid., 115.
9. Peter Berger, *The Heretical Imperative: Contemporary Possibilities of Religious Affirmation* (Garden City, N.Y.: Doubleday, 1980), 24.

that religious truth-claims should be subjected to the scrutiny of history and other empirical disciplines. And Berger is confident that when this occurs it will become clear how well religions address the full scope of basic human needs.[10]

Newbigin rejects this requirement. To insist that religious claims must be subjected to this sort of vindication is to allow the scientific perspective to gain a privileged position; in Berger's account, Newbigin argues, the empirical sciences are themselves exempted from the tests to which religions are subjected, and are at the same time immunized against religious critique:

> Here pluralism is not accepted. No question is raised here about the presuppositions upon which these scientific disciplines operate. No place is given to the possibility that what was given in the religious experience could provide an insight into truth that might radically relativize the presuppositions of the scientific disciplines.[11]

Newbigin's commitment to a religious critique of cultures is clearly at work here. The Christian message, he claims, is first of all a critical force calling into question every culture. This is why he attacks the arguments used by secularists to shield the public realm from the criticism that arises out of specific visions of the good life:

> No state can be completely secular in the sense that those who exercise power have no beliefs about what is true and no commitments to what they believe to be right. It is the duty of the church to ask what those beliefs and commitments are and to expose them to the light of the gospel.[12]

10. Ibid., 136.
11. Newbigin, *Foolishness to the Greeks,* 17-18.
12. Ibid., 132.

This critique is on the whole a cogent one. Newbigin certainly probes some vulnerable points in the kind of perspective set forth by Rawls and Novak. But we must also ask whether Newbigin successfully safeguards the public realm from the dangers posed by the clash between competing visions of the good.

Is the public-private distinction nothing but the invention of those secularists who want to drive a wedge that will separate religion from public life? Or can the dichotomy also be seen as arising out of a proper concern to protect commonality and mutuality in a day when such commodities are increasingly difficult to come by? Is there not a distinctively public sphere that does need protection from those forces that would destroy it? Finally, how much pluralism can this realm sustain without losing its public character?

A PUBLIC ETHIC

Richard Neuhaus deals with these questions by minimizing their relevance to a proper understanding of the public square. He treats appeals to pluralism primarily as a facade behind which liberals hide relativistic tendencies. His own search for a public ethic is explicitly intended as an alternative to such a liberalism. This is not to say that he sees all references to pluralism as a mere diversionary tactic. Neuhaus does want to allow for a measure of diverse convictions within the public ethic. But his treatment of this diversity is characterized, as we shall see, by some important ambiguities. Neuhaus is convinced that many people focus on the fact of conflicting convictions because they want to "count all opinions about morality as equal."[13] The liberal insistence on the significance of pluralism functions as a dogma that leaves no

13. Neuhaus, *Naked Public Square*, 111.

room for other dogmas; this is why pluralism is such a "jealous god." But again: Neuhaus does not reject pluralistic analyses as such. He even endorses Allan Bloom's complaint that the fashionable contemporary celebration of cultural diversity only serves to divert our attention from "*real differences* in fundamental beliefs about good and evil, about what is highest, about God."[14]

In spite of this endorsement, however, Neuhaus usually keeps even these "real differences" in the background. For example, while he allows that Alasdair MacIntyre "may be right" in insisting that we have already reached the point where politics has become a form of civil warfare, Neuhaus proceeds to argue for the availability of a public ethic that is grounded in religious convictions.[15] Public discourse, he argues, requires those people who do not share the same religious beliefs to employ a common moral language that might mediate between them. It is the role of a public ethic to develop this common discourse.[16]

This public philosophy, Neuhaus argues, must itself be sensitive to religious questions; this is inescapable, since the issues of our common life cannot be discussed in ignorance of the religious dimensions of the American experience.[17] To support this contention he shows how Adams, Tocqueville, and Lincoln stressed the ways in which public discourse relies on values that are religiously grounded.[18]

Neuhaus contends that America is still very much an

14. Allan Bloom, *The Closing of the American Mind* (New York: Simon and Schuster, 1987), 192. For Neuhaus's endorsement see the September 1987 issue of *Religion and Society Report*.

15. Neuhaus, *Naked Public Square*, 21.

16. Richard J. Neuhaus, "From Civil Religion to Public Philosophy," in *Civil Religion and Political Theology*, ed. Leroy S. Rouner, Boston University Studies in Philosophy and Religion, vol. 8 (Notre Dame, Ind.: University of Notre Dame Press, 1986), 107.

17. Ibid., 106.

18. Neuhaus, *Naked Public Square*, 145.

unsecular nation: "the overwhelming majority of Americans identify self-confessed religion as the morality-bearing component in culture."[19] Nor does Neuhaus shrink from the more specific conclusion that the majority endorses the religion of the Hebrew and Christian Scriptures; "the raw demographic reality" is, he judges, that a majority of Americans hold ideals and values based upon the biblical tradition.[20]

CRITICAL PATRIOTISM

America's "unsecularity" is an obvious strength in Neuhaus's scheme. It provides the basis for a "critical patriotism," as opposed to an uncompromising national chauvinism. This type of critical national identity nurtures a sense of what it means to be "a nation under God." To think of one's political community as existing under divine judgment

> means most importantly that there is a transcendent point of reference to which we as a people are accountable. It means there is an acknowledged framework within which criticism does not destroy community and protest is not the enemy of patriotism. In the naked public square there is no agreed-upon authority that is higher than the community itself. There is no publicly recognizable source for such criticism nor check upon such patriotism. Therefore criticism becomes impossible and patriotism unsafe.[21]

Against those who fear that a close linkage between religion and public life would encourage intolerance and uniformity, Neuhaus argues that the real enemies of a public

19. Neuhaus, "From Providence to Privacy," 63.
20. Neuhaus, *Naked Public Square,* 139.
21. Ibid., 76.

dialogue characterized by a healthy give-and-take are the promoters of "value-neutrality." Their hoped-for naked public square would sooner or later show its real intolerant face: in the absence of an impartial, transcendent point of reference the criterion for what is tolerable becomes a matter of what best serves the survival of the whole.

Needless to say, Neuhaus is well aware of the dangers posed by his more intolerant co-religionists — people who would denounce his own brand of "critical patriotism" as "weak-kneed accommodationism." It is unfortunate, he thinks, that the presence of this brand of religious dogmatism, which regularly confuses its own formulations of the truth with the divine truth itself, obscures an important principle: namely, that only a communal acceptance of "transcendent accountability" can provide us with the kind of "modesty and provisionality" necessary for sustaining the democratic spirit.[22]

DIVERSITY AND DIVINE PURPOSE

Neuhaus does not seem to be opposed to religious diversity as such. For example, he understands the Apostle Paul's treatment of the relation between Jews and Christians to be suggesting "that diversity in belief is inherent in, and not accidental to, the divine purpose."[23] This line of argument, if applied consistently to the full range of religious diversity, would certainly go far toward removing the plurality of religious perspectives from the realm of the mere "contingent" — which is, of course, where Rawls wants to keep religious belief.

Yet it is not clear that Neuhaus succeeds in this removal operation. Having acknowledged religious diversity as an

22. Ibid., 122-124.
23. Ibid., 122.

enduring presence in public life, it would be appropriate for Neuhaus to discuss how the interaction between diverse religious perspectives might be structured in the public square. But unfortunately he pays virtually no attention to the kinds of rules and procedures that are necessary for adjudicating public conflict. Instead he concentrates almost exclusively on the reasons why governments should not be expected to adjudicate this conflict in an effective manner. Nakedness cannot be a lasting feature of the public square, in Neuhaus's view, because governments will inevitably make judgments about the ultimate issues of life — and will thereby invade the realm of religion. Politics, then, is itself religious because of its inherent impulse toward dominance.

It is not wrongheaded to raise this concern. We do need to be reminded of governmental tendencies to overstep proper bounds. But this reminder can be effective only if we acknowledge that governments do *have* proper bounds within which to operate. And this is precisely where Neuhaus's account fails to shed light. He tells us little about what happens when political authority is being exercised in a legitimate and normal manner. And this too is an important topic to consider when we are investigating the role of religion in public life.

In his own way, then, Neuhaus treats religious influences as if they were a contingent presence in public life. Much of his analysis relies on his assertion that the United States *happens* to be an "unsecular" nation, since the majority of the people do not in fact accept "nakedness" as the normal condition of the public square. Much that is crucial to Neuhaus's case rests on his assessment of the "raw demographic reality" of a specific national situation. What he fails to provide is a systematic analysis of the proper relationships between religion and politics and the public square as such. Because of this failure, his case has little application to, say, the Netherlands or England or Canada — which is unfortunate since the issues he discusses also have relevance for other national contexts.

PLURALISM WITHIN COMMONALITY

Still, we must push this line of criticism further. At a crucial level of political concern, where the questions about the meaning and ends of government are being debated, religious perspectives play a minimal role in Neuhaus's scheme. At a crucial point in his account, religious viewpoints on issues of public life give way to a communal allegiance to American democracy.

Neuhaus does see a legitimate role for pluralism in public life. But this role is carefully circumscribed. Pluralism functions, for Neuhaus, within a set of larger communal loyalties. Indeed, Neuhaus proposes a kind of "litmus test" for deciding whether someone exhibits the appropriate form of critical patriotism. The test is whether or not assent can be given to this "carefully nuanced proposition: *On balance and considering the alternatives, the influence of the United States is a force for good in the world.*"[24] This empirical assessment is closely tied, in Neuhaus's scheme, to an acceptance of a sense of national mission whose formulation "will be strongly stamped by religion."[25]

And what of those who will resist this renewed emphasis on "Religious America"? They must be brought to understand that the very existence of the democratic experiment is at stake. Democracy requires a moral order, and this moral order must itself be derived from higher truth-claims that are inevitably religious in nature.[26]

24. Ibid., 72.
25. Neuhaus, "From Providence to Privacy," 65.
26. Ibid.

Again, this larger set of loyalties and convictions serves to place important restrictions on the pluralism that can function in American society. A clear preference is given to those viewpoints that allow for a religious interpretation of America's mission and destiny; those who dissent from such an interpretation are bound to feel that they are being treated as second class citizens.

Neuhaus has a peculiar way of dealing with this sense of exclusion: he plays down the fact of disagreement. Noting, for example, that much attention has been given to the growing numbers of adherents to Islam and the Eastern religions in the United States, he discounts the relevance of this fact to the question of pluralism:

> There is no evidence to date . . . that these groups are, when it comes to the public order, doing anything other than accommodating their traditions to the cultural and constitutional arrangements that are, in largest part, derived from biblical religion.[27]

This is a typical move for Neuhaus; when confronted with the charge that non-Christian religious groups will be offended by the strongly Christian tone of his prescribed public philosophy, he tends to minimize the disagreements that those groups might have with his understanding of "Religious America."

It is not clear that his efforts in this regard are reassuring to the groups in question. In his review of *The Naked Public Square,* James Nuechterlein points, for example, to the problems that Jews might have with Neuhaus's perspective:

> If America's sacred canopy must be Judeo-Christian in content, what does this suggest for those outside that category?

---

27. Richard J. Neuhaus, "Genuine Pluralism and the Pfefferian Inversion," *This World,* no. 24 (Winter 1989): 83.

Are they not then excluded by definition from the social consensus binding society together? And Neuhaus's formulation is problematic even within its own terms: Jews and Christians, as Neuhaus well knows, have quite different conceptions of history's meaning and destiny, and the term "Judeo-Christian" is a convention that implies far more in the way of a common world view than is in fact the case.[28]

This is an important point. But even if Neuhaus could respond to it adequately — by spelling out, for example, a public philosophy that draws heavily on "Judeo-Christian" resources while remaining attractive to Jews and Christians, as well as Muslims, Hindus, and Buddhists — still he would not have provided us with an adequate account of pluralism in public life. What he would have shown is that the contingencies of the American situation are such that the challenge of pluralism is not as pressing as many people think it to be.

GOSPEL AND CONTEXT

For Newbigin, of course, Neuhaus's line of argument is of little help, since Newbigin is concerned primarily with situations in which Christians are an obvious minority. The two-pronged strategy of isolating the secularists by questioning the actual impact of secularization and claiming a strong public philosophical consensus among various religious groups will not serve his purposes very well. On the contrary, he simply takes it for granted that the public role of Christian religion is no longer self-evident.

---

28. James Nuechterlein, "A Sacred Canopy?" Review of *The Naked Public Square: Religion and Democracy in America,* by Richard John Neuhaus; in *Commentary* 79, no. 1 (Jan. 1985): 80.

On what grounds, then, does Newbigin attack the pub-lic-private dichotomy? What could be the public relevance of a religious outlook shared by a rather small segment of the population?

This is precisely where Newbigin's experience as a mis-sionary comes into play. He knows that when it comes to judging truth-claims, "raw demographic reality" can never be decisive. The fact that in modern society Christians have become one of the many minority groups has no bearing on an evaluation of the authority of the gospel. What the demo-graphic data do teach us is that the Christian's role in public life now resembles that of the missionary. In other words, what really counts, as all missionaries know, is the intrinsic quality of the message that is being proclaimed. The question, then, is whether the gospel has application to the issues of public life. Newbigin obviously thinks that it does.

On the other hand, the Christian message does have to be proclaimed and applied in order to become culturally relevant. This is crucial to what Newbigin explicitly refers to as the "missionary encounter."[29] And in order for there to be such an encounter, the gospel has to be articulated in terms that speak to the specific culture addressed. Newbigin knows the importance of cultural contexts:

> Neither at the beginning, nor at any subsequent time, is there or can there be a gospel that is not embodied in a culturally conditioned form of words. . . . Every statement of the gospel in words is conditioned by the culture of which those words are a part, and every style of life that claims to embody the truth of the gospel is a culturally conditioned style of life. There can never be a culture-free gospel.[30]

29. Newbigin, *Foolishness to the Greeks*, 132-133.
30. Ibid., 4.

Furthermore, to understand this fact of cultural-embedded-ness, it is necessary to see the importance of conscious efforts to make the Christian message culturally relevant. A genuine "encounter" requires an ability to address others in their own terms.

Yet won't this insistence on the importance of contextualization inevitably lead to a relativizing of the authority of the gospel? Newbigin thinks not: "the gospel, which is from the beginning to the end embodied in culturally conditioned forms, calls into question all cultures." Newbigin illustrates this contention by citing the example of the Apostle Paul's speech before King Agrippa, where Paul describes his experience of hearing God's voice on the Damascus road: "I heard a voice to me in Hebrew language . . ." (Acts 26:14). This, says Newbigin, is a good example of contextualization, for the message that changed Paul's life was spoken to him in his own native tongue. But neither was that the end of the matter. The intent of this act of divine contextualization was not to condone, but rather to challenge, Saul's present way of life: "Why do you persecute me?"[31]

The message of the gospel does not simply add a spiritual dimension to profane culture. It enters into our human contexts in order to judge, to challenge, and to transform. Newbigin thereby gives the historical conditions of the messengers their full due — but with every intention of avoiding relativism. The human messengers may not contextualize the gospel however they wish: they too stand under its judgment.

NEITHER SACRAL NOR SECULAR

Newbigin views human life in all of its private and public complexity as falling within the scope of the Kingdom of

31. Ibid., 4-5.

God. This is why he strongly resists Novak's "empty shrine" proposal. And it is also why he argues against those thinkers, including some Christian theologians, who virtually equate the "secularization" of public life with the emancipation of public institutions from ecclesiastical tutelage. While Newbigin wants to free public life from churchly control, he does not advocate the secularization of political life.

For one thing, the notion of a completely "secularized" public square is, in Newbigin's view, an illusion:

No state can be completely secular in the sense that those who exercise power have no beliefs about what is true and no commitments to what they believe to be right. It is the duty of the church to ask what those beliefs and commitments are and to expose them to the light of the gospel.[32]

But, furthermore, Newbigin is convinced that the choice between thoroughgoing secularization and a church-controlled society is a false one. If Newbigin rejects the secularization project, he also firmly opposes any "return to the era of the *corpus Christianum*," when the church was closely identified with the political authorities. Citing the example of Islamic fundamentalism, Newbigin insists that the "sacralizing" of political life "always unleashes demonic powers."[33]

Newbigin is clear, then, about the alternatives he rejects. Both the notion that public life can function in a religiously neutral manner and the ideal of an ecclesiocentric social order are defective. But what are we to put in place of these two options? His own conception of the proper way of construing the relationship between Christianity and public life is not developed in any detail. But he does offer a few clues as to what he has in mind.

32. Ibid., 132.
33. Ibid., 115-116.

For example, Newbigin does not seem to be principally opposed to the idea of a "Christian state." Ideally, he thinks, it should be possible to establish a state "that acknowledges the Christian faith as true, but deliberately provides full security for those of other views."[34] He even seems to think that a substantive commitment to Christian tenets is necessary for the health of the public square — the church must make it clear, he tells us at one point, "that the central shrine of a nation's life cannot remain empty, that if Christ is not there then an idol will certainly take his place."[35]

This does not mean, however, that the church should impose its convictions on people who do not accept its gospel. Indeed, Newbigin does not see the church, in the sense of an institutionalized body, as having a direct role in the formation of public policy. Implementing the kind of vision he has in mind is the task of the laity who, equipped with a "declericalized" theology, will "seek illumination from the gospel for their daily secular duty."[36]

This way of relating Christian convictions to the public square will take on the character, for Newbigin, of a "missionary encounter with our culture"[37] in which Christians "enter into a genuinely listening dialogue" with non-Christians, a conversation in which Christians take it for granted that they have much to learn from those with whom they disagree.[38] Only a spirit of humble openness can keep Christians from establishing their own form of totalitarianism.

Again, Newbigin is doing little more here than providing some rudimentary clues to how his alternative perspective might be developed. His brief sketch, while provocative and promising, leaves many questions unanswered. The ques-

34. Ibid., 140.
35. Ibid., 123.
36. Ibid., 141-143.
37. Ibid., 141.

tions, though, are crucial ones to be addressed by people who are sympathetic to his overall project.

What exactly does it mean, for example, to place Christ at the center — in "the central shrine" — of public life? And could Newbigin's arrangement be in any way construed as a *just* solution to the problems engendered by an increasing pluralism? Does it allow for a higher degree of justice than Rawls's scheme? And could the arena in which Newbigin's "missionary encounter" takes place rightly be thought of as a *public* space? These are the topics that we will pursue in a more thematic fashion in the subsequent chapters.

⊶ 4 ⊷

The Quest for Public Selfhood

ACCORDING TO Richard Sennett, modern industrial society has lost an appropriate sense of the benefits of public civility. Our contemporary obsession with intimate warmth in human affairs amounts to what Sennett labels an "ideology of intimacy," which views "social relationships of all kinds [as] real, believable, and authentic the closer they approach the inner psychological concerns of each person." This perspective, Sennett argues, "transmutes political categories into psychological categories."[1]

This transmutation leaves us, according to Sennett, with a lack of appreciation for the kinds of "bonds of association and mutual commitment which exist between people who are not joined together by ties of family or intimate association"; we have lost our sense of the value of "the bond of a crowd, of a 'people,' of a polity."[2] This loss of public selfhood creates, in turn, private disruption: "confusion has arisen between public and intimate life; people are working

1. Richard Sennett, *The Fall of Public Man: On the Social Psychology of Capitalism* (New York: Random House, Vintage Books, 1978), 259.
2. Ibid., 3-4.

out in terms of personal feelings public matters which properly can be dealt with only through codes of impersonal meaning."[3]

In short, what we have lost in all of this, as Sennett sees things, is a proper sense of the meaning of the city itself:

> "City" and "civility" have a common root etymologically. Civility is treating others as though they were strangers and forging a social bond upon that social distance. The city is that human settlement in which strangers are most likely to meet. The public geography of a city is civility institution alized.[4]

MODERNITY AND PUBLIC CONSCIOUSNESS

In the previous chapter we noted Lesslie Newbigin's critical comments regarding "the division between the private world and the public"[5] — a dichotomy that Newbigin takes to be "one of the outstanding marks of a 'modern' society."[6] On a quick reading of Newbigin's account, he might appear to be disagreeing with Sennett's analysis on at least two points. First, Newbigin seems to be saying that a clear distinction between public and private has not been lost to modernity, but is actually a distinguishing feature of the modern consciousness. And second, Newbigin seems to think that the public-private dichotomy is one that we would all be better off without.

The apparent differences between Newbigin's and Sennett's accounts fade, however, when we take a closer look at what Newbigin is actually criticizing in the public-versus-

3. Ibid., 5.
4. Ibid., 264.
5. Newbigin, *Foolishness to the Greeks,* 18-19.
6. Ibid., 35.

private distinction. He is not opposed to the distinction between public and private as such. Rather, he focuses on the way in which this distinction is used to reinforce a rigid bifurcation between "fact" and "value," where

> [t]he public world is a world of facts that are the same for everyone, whatever his values may be; the private world is a world of values where all are free to choose their own values and therefore to pursue such courses of action as will correspond with them.[7]

It is not necessary for our discussion to determine whether the analyses offered by Sennett and Newbigin are compatible. But there is one fairly straightforward way of reconciling their accounts — a way that also has the benefit of providing a fairly accurate rendering of the problematic status of the public-private distinction in contemporary life.

Newbigin rightly emphasizes the fact that the public and private dichotomy has been regularly used in modern thought to reinforce a strict fact-value bifurcation. This rigid dichotomy is unfortunate, for it does not provide human beings with a satisfactory way of achieving public selfhood. Therefore many people attempt to privatize the public, a project whose inadequacies Sennett deftly exposes. Another option that is sometimes pursued — one that Sennett does not discuss — is the attempt to publicize the private: for example, when the marital relationship is portrayed primarily in corporate-legal ("marriage contract") and political ("sexual politics") terms.[8]

---

7. Ibid., 36.
8. For a helpful summary of the theoretical basis for this publicizing-of-the-private pattern in the Marxist strand of recent feminism, see Josephine Donovan, *Feminist Theory: The Intellectual Traditions of American Feminism* (New York: Frederick Ungar Publishing Co., 1985), ch. 3, especially 75-80.

THE BENEFITS OF PUBLIC SPACE

Still, why worry about preserving a clear distinction between public and private selfhood? Why is it a good thing to maintain those "codes of impersonal meaning" that Sennett associates with public interaction?

In his recent study of psychiatric patients, James M. Glass offers a similar perspective to Sennett's on the benefits of a public consciousness. Glass, a political theorist, spent considerable time with persons classified as mentally ill to investigate the ways in which they find themselves unable to participate in communal realities. The patients whom Glass studied were each immersed, he sensed, "in the flows of an internal nature that leaves the self isolated, sometimes psychotic, and withdrawn from consensual relationship."[9] They lacked a properly developed *public* selfhood; their struggle for health was in effect a grasping for a firmer hold on "existence-in-common" and "intersubjectivity." Thus, Glass argues, "the discourse between the self and its public field may constitute experience of considerable benefit for a consciousness desperately fighting the entropic pull of tyrannical inner images."[10]

Both Sennett and Glass, then, are convinced of the therapeutic benefits afforded by public selfhood. Where incivility holds sway, says Sennett, each of us must bear the "burden of personality"; civility, on the other hand, "has as its aim the shielding of others from being burdened with oneself."[11] Glass puts it even more poignantly: our citizenship roles facilitiate "the persistent *public* mediation of private hells and inner conflicts."[12]

This desire for the kinds of public interactions that can

9. James M. Glass, *Private Terror/Public Life: Psychosis and the Politics of Community* (Ithaca, N.Y.: Cornell University Press, 1989), 14.
10. Ibid., 26.
11. Sennett, *Fall of Public Man*, 264-265, 269.
12. Glass, *Private Terror/Public Life*, 27.

facilitate the integration of our individual experiences has a parallel in the call by Robert Bellah and his associates for a public integration of social scientific discourse. The authors of *Habits of the Heart* and *The Good Society* are interested in delineating the conditions that would facilitate a much-needed opening up of our communal "spaces for reflection, participation, and the transformation of our institutions." And they are convinced that the "specialists and experts" who engage in the academic study of society have an important contribution to make to this development.[13]

The nature and scope of this hoped-for contribution is laid out in some detail in an appendix to *Habits of the Heart*. This essay, entitled "Social Science as Public Philosophy," calls for the kind of scholarly address to questions of public life that is "concerned with the whole of society"; such an address would present a "synoptic view" of corporate life that would be "at once philosophical, historical, and socio-logical." This contribution would require, the Bellah team insists, the restoration of the older conception of social scientific investigation as an exercise in public philosophy.[14]

13. Robert Bellah et al., *Habits of the Heart: Individualism and Com-mitment in American Life* (Berkeley, Calif.: University of California Press, 1985), 218, 303. See also *The Good Society* (New York, N.Y.: Alfred A. Knopf, 1991); *The Good Society* is a sequel to *Habits of the Heart* in that it continues the critique of the "Lockean individualism" that *Habits of the Heart* saw as eroding our commitments to each other and to the common good. *The Good Society* probes for the effects of individualism in American economic, social, religious, and political institutions. The prognosis offered here is not good. The fear expressed by the authors is that we have become rich as individuals and poor as a society. Like *Habits of the Heart, The Good Society* is not utterly pessimistic about the prospects of restoring a healthy com-monweal. Both books see the need for a recovery of meaning and com-mitment as much in our social and political institutions as in the moral convictions of individuals. But successful renewal will only be accomplished by a rediscovery of the "communities of memory" found in the biblical and civic republican traditions. We are treating the two works here as setting forth these common themes.

14. Ibid., 298, 302.

72

On the Bellah team's reading of the present state of social scientific discussion, this process really would require a restoration of something that has been for the most part lost. While the public philosophy tradition has not completely disappeared, they observe, "it has been driven to the periphery by an ever more specialized social science whose sub-disciplines often cannot speak to one another, much less to the public."[15]

The Bellah team does not use the graphic language that Glass employs in describing the plight of his psychiatric patients. The authors of *Habits of the Heart* do not insist, for example, that contemporary social scientists are trapped in "private hells and inner conflicts." But they do think that the social scientific status quo is in a serious state of fragmentation. And they are not alone in their worries. In his masterful 1963 study of political thought, Sheldon Wolin complained of a widespread social scientific "localism" that accepts a "picture of society as a series of tight little islands, each evolving towards political self-sufficiency, each striving to absorb the individual members, each without any natural affiliations with a more comprehensive unity."[16]

These calls for an integrating perspective in both our private lives and our understandings of the broader patterns of social interaction are significant ones. It is worth exploring what it would take to restore a healthier sense of public selfhood, and worth looking at what Christian thought and practice might be able to contribute to this restorative project.

---

15. Ibid., 299.
16. Sheldon S. Wolin, *Politics and Vision: Continuity and Innovation in Western Political Thought* (Boston: Little, Brown and Co., 1960), 431.

INTENDING THE COMMON GOOD

What exactly are we talking about when we ask about a healthy sense of public selfhood? It isn't easy to come up with a clear set of reference points for answering this question. For one thing, there isn't an extensive body of literature to draw upon; most discussions of issues pertaining to public thought and practice fail to offer a clarification of their use of the term "public." Furthermore, not all of the writers who bemoan the loss of a sense of public selfhood are operating with exactly the same understandings of what would be included in a healthy understanding of public life.

Most thinkers who are concerned about this topic are in agreement, however, that a proper public consciousness requires the intentional pursuit of the common good. To insist on *intentionality* in this regard is to reject the Hobbesian conviction that a public-type interaction can be sustained without a subjective publicly-oriented outlook supported by the actors involved. The Hobbesian approach places the sole responsibility for promoting a public atmosphere on the decision-making system itself. On this view, it is not necessary for people who participate in public debates to concentrate on anything other than their own "factional" projects. It is the function of the policy-making system to coordinate these diverse passions into relatively harmonious policies by submitting factional advocacies to the discipline of a systemic taming process. The qualities that we might associate with public life are to be found in the policies produced and not in the psyches of the persons who produce them.

To reject this Hobbesian perspective is to insist that systemic features alone cannot succeed in creating a proper sphere of public interaction. It is to recognize that public consciousness requires the cultivation of those subjective dispositions that Rawls describes as the "*very great* virtues," such as "the virtues of tolerance and being ready to meet

74

others halfway, and the virtue of reasonableness and the sense of fairness."[17]

The exercise of these virtues will be inadequate for a healthy public consciousness, though, without a conception of the *common good* as that which is intended by the public self. A spirit of cooperation, fair-mindedness, and toleration must be directed toward the pursuit of shared goals — the fulfilling of those interests that work toward the actual well-being of the larger community.

Again, this sense of the common good as that toward which our best efforts are intentionally directed is a crucial one. As David Hollenbach has observed in criticizing Michael Novak's "free market" conception of public life, it is not to accept the common good as too complex a notion for anyone to grasp, recommending instead the fair-minded pursuit of self-interested goals. Such strategies will not necessarily promote a set of shared interests, nor will such efforts necessarily promote whatever the common good turns out to be. Hollenbach insists that a conscious reckoning with the common good must be a part of social planning, since the determination of appropriate goals and objectives necessitates our "attending carefully to the way they are connected to the larger goals of society as a whole."[18]

THE CONSENSUS STRAND

In spite of agreement on these basic and important matters, however, thinkers who are concerned about a healthy public selfhood work with differing notions of what a viable pattern of public interaction would look like. For our purposes it

17. Rawls, "Overlapping Consensus," 17.
18. David Hollenbach, S.J., "The Common Good Revisited," *Theological Studies* 50 (1989), 73.

will suffice to distinguish between two major strands of "public philosophy." The first of these strands places a strong emphasis on the need for ultimate consensus in public life. This consensus strand is recognizable to anyone familiar with contemporary discussions of religious pluralism. Indeed, we have already encountered expressions of this perspective at several points in our discussion. On this view a healthy public life is one wherein people acknowledge those things that they have in common in spite of their other differences — such as differing religious convictions. The concern here is to keep all controversial items out of the public realm. This strand of thinking fits well with an Enlightenment perspective in which the public arena is viewed as the domain of reason, while appeals to revelation are consigned to the terrain of private belief.

The consensus strand is nicely developed in Walter Lippmann's *The Public Philosophy*. Lippmann's concern, accentuated by the events of the 1930s and '40s, was that democratic politics was becoming a mere plaything of public opinion. Lippmann illustrates his concern with the example of changing attitudes toward Nazi Germany on the part of the United States: at first the general public did not want to go to war; during the war it could be satisfied with nothing short of Germany's unconditional surrender; then after the war interest in the observance of the peace accords quickly dissipated. All of this signalled, for Lippmann, a lack of a compass. Western democracies had lost their grasp of "the public philosophy."[19]

This philosophy — and Lippmann deliberately uses the singular — rests on universal and unchanging principles that are grounded in natural law.[20] These principles come to

19. Walter Lippmann, *The Public Philosophy* (Boston: Little, Brown and Co., 1955), 25-27.
20. Ibid., 79-85.

expression, though, under differing historical circumstances. Thus the one public philosophy is embedded in a variety of "traditions of civility." These traditions are necessary in actualizing human qualities. To develop a proper concern for public interaction is, as Walter Lippmann makes the case, to realize our "second and civilized nature." It means achieving "the inwardness of the ruling man," who has gained power over his less social instincts and affections "for the sake of his realm, of his order, of his regiment, of his ship, of his cause."[21] When a society's civilized adherence to firm principles begins to weaken, according to Lippmann, privatization sets in. All strong convictions are banned to the realm of private consciousness; the result is a minimal pseudo-consensus, with little to protect the citizenry from the inroads of totalitarianism.

Lippmann's remedy for an unhealthy privatization is to stress the need for a single, relatively unified, "public philosophy." The Christian religion can make a contribution to the maintenance of this philosophy by functioning as one of several "traditions of civility" — which necessitates that all of the more controversial aspects of Christian teaching will remain matters of private conviction. Religious diversity, then, does have some contribution to make to public life — namely, to offer a variety of reinforcements for civil discourse. It is philosophical unity, however, and not plurality, that is the desired goal.

THE PLURALITY STRAND

At about the same time that Lippmann published *The Public Philosophy,* Hannah Arendt was working intensely on the theme of public and private. In rudimentary form her treat-

21. Ibid., 107.

ment is already present in *The Origins of Totalitarianism,* but the more fully developed version is found in *The Human Condition.* Her position nicely illustrates the second strand in public philosophy discussions, one that places a strong emphasis on the importance of plurality in public life.

Like Lippmann, Arendt operates with the republican ideal of the *polis* as that community wherein free citizens collectively look after the *res publica.* Where she differs from Lippmann is in her deep commitment to plurality: in the *polis* we meet each other as equals, with the recognition of our diversity being an important part of our public consciousness.

This celebration of diversity is crucial to Arendt's notion of "public space." The central space of the *polis* is not for her an imaginary intersection in which we realize pure consensus; it is an arena in which distinctions are maintained as we communicate with each other while preserving our unique identities. It is only in such a space that true individuality can flourish, because only there do continuity and distinction, communality and separation, mingle together.[22]

Richard Bernstein illuminates this use of the spatial metaphor in his summary of Arendt's understanding of the proper conditions for public consciousness: Human life is sustained in action and speech. Action and speech, in turn, require human plurality, because they have to occur *in between* human beings, as one unique human being encounters the "otherness" of human plurality. Action, as the realization of our humanness, necessarily takes place, then, in the public space of the *polis* — the arena in which we reveal — both to ourselves and to others — who we are.[23]

This "revelatory" dimension of public interaction is crucial

22. Hannah Arendt, *The Human Condition* (Chicago: University of Chicago Press, 1958), 52-53.
23. Richard J. Bernstein, *Beyond Objectivism and Relativism: Science, Hermeneutics, and Praxis* (Philadelphia: University of Pennsylvania Press, 1983), 208.

to Arendt. She sees the basic distinction between private and public as residing in the fact "that there are things that need to be hidden and others that need to be displayed publicly if they are to exist at all";[24] citing classical conceptions of human excellence, she notes that activities that are appropriately performed in the public realm

> can attain an excellence never matched in privacy; for excellence, by definition, the presence of others is always required, and this presence needs the formality of the public, constituted by one's peers, it cannot be the casual, familiar presence of one's equals or inferiors.[25]

Arendt is not very clear, however, about how the encounter between genuinely diverse perspectives on human life will actually promote public health. Indeed, on the question of religious diversity she is not very helpful at all, since she does not seem to think that a religion like Christianity has any public role to play; the religion of Jesus is, in her view, a nonpolitical, nonpublic bond of spiritual kinship.[26]

Furthermore, the plurality that she does welcome into the public arena does not actually constitute, in her mind, a multiplicity of viewpoints that are at bottom irreconcilable. It is not insignificant that "space" is her favorite metaphor for the public domain. Public plurality is finally, for Arendt, a kind of spatial-perspectival diversity. Seemingly basic differences of conviction have to do with the fact that the issues of human reality are seen from a variety of perspectives. Political debate allows us to gain the larger picture by considering other perspectives.[27]

24. Arendt, *The Human Condition,* 73.
25. Ibid., 49.
26. See, e.g., ibid., 35, 53, 60, 74.
27. Ibid., 57.

THE SCOPE OF THE PUBLIC DOMAIN

One topic that needs to be clarified in these explorations of public selfhood is the question of how widely we must construe the scope of the public domain. People who write about public consciousness sometimes give the impression that the public is coextensive with the political. But this does not address certain other interactions often thought of as falling within our "public" life. As both the forum and the arena where matters of general interest are considered, the public domain encompasses more than political interaction. For example, the "op-ed" pages of a newspaper are rightly thought of as a public forum even though the topics discussed — such as crowd behavior at sports events, racial and gender stereotypes in advertising, religious bigotry — range more widely than the political.

Public life, then, cannot be contained within the boundaries of politics. A political system links the citizen to the state by means of a representational system and political parties. But the larger public realm comprises all that pertains to the common good, from public services rendered by the government to many of the activities associated with universities, corporations, churches, charitable foundations, and the like.

There are good reasons for emphasizing this more-than-political character of the public realm. Consider, for example, Richard Neuhaus's observation regarding the American political system:

> The constitutional polity was not intended to bear the burden of cultivating virtue. Indeed virtue was outside the sphere of the polity, but not outside the sphere of what is public. The force of virtue was thought to be both prior to and reinforcing of the polity. The polity presupposed a

80

culture of virtue; it was not intended to replace it and it could not create a new one in its place.[28]

This is a significant observation. A society's polity does not constitute an autonomous field that can nurture and sustain its own public character without help from the outside. It shares the public realm with a variety of other systems and institutions. Nonpolitical resources are indispensable for the formation of a healthy public consciousness. Indeed, the threat of totalitarianism emerges precisely when these other resources are ignored or cut off.

It should be obvious that neither Lippmann nor Arendt is concerned to place severe restrictions on the scope of public interaction. Lippmann places a high value on the contribution that various "traditions of civility," including religious ones, can make to public life. And Arendt insists that we bring our individual differences with us into the space of public interaction.

Yet each of them operates with a rather limited understanding of the public domain. One obvious indication of this has to do with the role that is assigned to Christianity in each of their schemes. Lippmann wants to limit the Christian contribution to the reinforcement of that which is common to diverse civility-traditions. And Arendt sees Christianity as having nothing much to say to the issues that are proper to a healthy public space.

But religious diversity is not the only factor that Lippmann and Arendt want to leave out of the public domain. The family is also excluded. The tradition of public philosophy that Lippmann and Arendt are attempting to reclaim is the one whose passing Sennett mourns when he describes a time when people valued "a life passed outside the life of family

28. Neuhaus, *The Naked Public Square*, 141.

and close friends," in a "public region" where "diverse, complex social groups were to be brought into ineluctable contact."[29] In this tradition, the family is part of the "natural" substratum that we must transcend if we are to become citizens. Like religious practice, a concern with familial ties has for these writers no place in the realm of public interaction.

CONVICTION AND KINSHIP IN PUBLIC LIFE

We noted earlier that Bellah and his co-authors call for a restoration of public philosophy. But it is clear in the light of the issues we have been discussing that the Bellah group actually disagrees on some important matters with past treatments of public philosophy and the nature of a healthy public space. For one thing, the Bellah team insists that genuine religious diversity has a positive contribution to make in the public square. They are convinced that it is precisely because public life has lost its grounding in the older religious and civic visions that the space devoted to public dialogue has become so crowded with individual interests. What is needed to correct this situation is the recovery and/or reinforcement of those "communities of memory" — especially those represented by the churches and synagogues — where, as the Bellah group puts it, "there are still operating among us . . . traditions that tell us about the nature of the world, about the nature of society, and about who we are as people."[30] These traditions — these communal memories — are, according to the case set forth in both *Habits of the Heart* and *The Good Society*, crucial to the health of a society.

Nor is the Bellah group interested in religion only insofar

29. Sennett, *Fall of Public Man*, 17.
30. Bellah, *Habits of the Heart*, 239, 281-282.

as it contributes to unity in public life. In a very un-Rawlsian manner they insist that a "thin political consensus" would do little to cure our social ills. Instead they take for granted a lasting diversity of irreconcilable starting-points and conflicting convictions in the public debate.[31]

Similarly, Bellah and his colleagues refuse simply to relegate familial ties to the realm of the "private." As we shall see in chapter 6, they make a strong plea for the public promotion of a rich associational diversity in contemporary life, in which a variety of nonpolitical groups contribute themes and concerns that will enhance public interaction. The Bellah group obviously thinks that a strong sense of public bonding will necessarily build upon, and draw strength from, the patterns of bonding that are experienced in nonpublic spheres of interaction. Thus, for example, the familial motif of "kinship" looms large in their discussion of public life.

There is a very good reason why the Bellah group is more inclined than other writers to see both religious and familial associations as having an important contribution to make to our understanding of a healthy public domain. Bellah and his colleagues are convinced that the increasing individualism has reached crisis proportions. People are less capable than they were in the past of articulating a commitment to something beyond the individual self. At the heart of this problem is a fundamental difficulty in thinking or speaking about interpersonal and community relations as having intrinsic meaning.

As the Bellah team views things, contemporary human beings do not merely have a problem with the bonds of citizenship — they have a problem with bonding as such. In this regard the Bellah team presents a more nuanced case than Sennett's, since they see contemporary people as having

31. Ibid., 246, 287, 301.

problems with both the more intimate and the more public patterns of interaction. The relationships appropriate to the *polis* are desperately in need of direct reinforcement from other more primal patterns of association. Yet these more intimate bonds are themselves — like our public interactions — threatened by an increasing individualization of both our consciousness and our discourse.

A PLURALITY OF DIVERSITIES

The Bellah discussion of what makes for health in the public arena points the way to issues that we want to explore at greater length in subsequent chapters. The two items just mentioned have a special relevance to our discussion. By emphasizing the importance of kinship ties for public life the Bellah group is insisting on the significance of associational diversity for public philosophy. And by stressing the value of religious differences for public dialogue they are suggesting an important role for directional pluralism.

Furthermore, the contribution of the Bellah group does not merely consist in the fact that they point to interesting topics. Their discussions also provide fascinating clues as to how these themes should be developed. For example, associational diversity is, according to the Bellah team, not merely valuable as a strategy for combatting individualism. On the contrary, "communal ties and religious commitments" have a kind of "grounding in reality."[32] They reflect a metaphysical "givenness"[33] that we must respect if we want to avoid a "purely contractual ethic [that] leaves every commitment unstable."[34]

32. Bellah, *Habits of the Heart,* 137.
33. Ibid., 140.
34. Ibid., 130.

An association such as the family, then, is a well-grounded given in the Bellah scheme. And religious conviction, too, runs deep in this portrayal of social reality. The Bellah group treats religious disagreement very seriously as an area manifesting profound and irreconcilable differences. These are important suggestions. Yet we must try to clarify the nature of the givenness of associational diversity. And we must look more closely at the question of directional diversity. On this latter topic, for example, the Bellah discussion leaves some interesting questions unanswered. What is going on when the Bellah group calls for an ongoing public "conversation, an argument in the best sense, about the meaning and value of our common life"?[35] In one sense, *The Good Society* is an attempt by Bellah and his colleagues to begin just such a conversation by focusing on the loss of directional potency in our political, religious, familial, and economic institutions. But when Bellah advocates, in a recent article, a "Niebuhrian dialectic of affirmation and humble recognition of one's finiteness,"[36] is he deemphasizing the significance of directional diversity? Is he in fact arguing, in a manner similar to Arendt, that directional differences are due in the final analysis to the fact that we view the same reality from a variety of finite spatial-type perspectives? And what would be an alternative view that would better preserve the depth-character of these differences?

We turn now to some of these difficult topics. To do this, we will make extensive use of the threefold scheme that we sketched out in the first chapter, where we distinguished among *directional, associational,* and *contextual* pluralism. Each of these types of pluralism deals with a specific kind

35. Ibid., 303.
36. Robert Bellah, "Public Philosophy and Public Theology," in *Civil Religion and Political Theology,* Boston University Studies in Philosophy and Religion, vol. 8, ed. Leroy S. Rouner (Notre Dame, Ind.: University of Notre Dame, 1986), 87.

of "cluttering" that occurs in public life, and each cluttering is regularly a subject for discussion in various treatments of pluralism — although the types are seldom clearly distinguished.[37] The complaint that the public arena is constricted by the presence of diverse directional — religious, philosophical, ideological — visions is obviously a frequent one. But people also worry about the ways in which diverse associational roles — those associated with our memberships in families, unions, corporations, and the like — impinge on our loyalties to the larger public. And a concern about the implications for public life of the plurality of culturally contextualized perspectives and experiences is becoming a high priority item on the contemporary agenda.

We will now discuss these types in more detail, devoting a chapter to each type of pluralism.

37. Paul Mojzes seems to have a similar classificatory scheme to ours in mind when he introduces a symposium on religious pluralism with this statement: "Pluralism — religious, cultural, political, and other — is a *fact* of our contemporary world, both on the global scale and often on the level of specific societies." Paul Mojzes, "Universality and Uniqueness in the Context of Religious Pluralism: An Introduction," *Journal of Ecumenical Studies* 26, no. 1 (Winter 1989): 1.

✦ 5 ✦

Understanding
Directional Diversity

IN *The Peasant of the Garonne* Jacques Maritain draws a sharp distinction between two truths about the world:

> There is . . . an "ontosophic truth" about the world considered in its natural structures or in what properly constitutes it; in this sense we must say that the world is fundamentally good. And there is a "religious" or "mystical" truth about the world considered in its ambiguous relationship to the kingdom of God and the Incarnation.[1]

Maritain is suggesting that it is possible to discern two very different and basic patterns on display in the world: on the one hand a rich array of ontic structures and on the other a complex drama of grace and rebellion. His distinction corresponds closely to one that Calvinists often make between the order of creation and the order of sin and redemption.[2] Recognizing the appropriateness of such a distinction

---

1. Jacques Maritain, *The Peasant of the Garonne* (New York: Holt, Rinehart and Winston, 1968), 60.
2. See, for example, Albert M. Wolters, *Creation Regained: Biblical*

leads us to differentiate between associational pluralism, which deals with the variety of associational structures (family, team, business, church, state), and directional pluralism, which ranges over the diversity of "spiritual" orientations.

To be sure, these two "orders" are interwoven in reality: our associational structures serve diverse directional orientations and our spiritual visions take on associational shapes. Our task, then, is not only to distinguish but also to connect. In this chapter we examine directional diversity, in the next we turn to associational patterns. As we have already indicated, we will also devote a chapter to a third motif, that of contextual plurality.

WHY "DIRECTIONAL"?

At first glance the term "directional" might seem inappropriate for our purposes in this discussion. Unlike "structural" and "contextual" it does not occupy a major place in philosophical vocabulary. We have chosen it, though, not because of its philosophical merits, but because it is an apt rendering of some significant Christian themes. The Bible regularly refers to the difference between the godly and sinful "ways" and righteous and unrighteous "paths" (see, e.g., Pss. 1:1; 18:21; 23:3; 119:28).

Nor does this imagery deal with marginal issues from a biblical perspective. "Path" and "way" suggest comprehensive patterns of behavior; the picture is one of human beings following a single and definable course in spite of the various circumstances in which they might find themselves. This is so because the direction that people take in their lives depends more upon their response to the divine call

Basics for a Reformational Worldview (Grand Rapids, Mich.: Wm. B. Eerdmans Publ. Co., 1985), 48.

to obedience than it does on the vicissitudes of the ensuing journey. Our basic orientations, either God-honoring or God-dishonoring, are the steering factors for our life pilgrimages.

Christian anthropology cannot avoid seeing the duality of obedience versus rebellion as the basic conflict in human life. As Flannery O'Connor once put it: "everything works toward its true end or away from it, everything is ultimately saved or lost."[3] Needless to say, it is also necessary to allow for the complexities of real life. Many factors keep human beings from living out their fundamental choices with full consistency. The basic directions may be clear — God-honoring or God-dishonoring — but actual people often seem to be pulled in two directions at once.

Some thinkers are inclined to speak of the "religious" where we refer to the "directional." There is something to be said for that choice, especially if "religion" is taken in the very general sense of someone's orientation toward the divine reality. Unfortunately, however, the word "religious" is regularly used in a much narrower sense, to refer to specifically religious institutions (churches, synagogues, temples, mosques) and concrete worshiping practices. To speak of "religious pluralism" with these connotations in mind is to address a narrower scope than the plurality of basic religious directions, in which the overall patterns of our lives are displayed.

UNBELIEF AS PLURALISTIC

The simple dichotomy between obedience and disobedience, however, is not by itself adequate for understanding the complexities of directional pluralism. It is both necessary and

3. Quoted by Frederick Crews, "The Power of Flannery O'Connor," *The New York Review of Books* 37, no. 7 (April 26, 1990): 51.

illuminating to pay some attention to the many different versions of unbelief.

St. Augustine noticed the varieties of unbelief in *Of True Religion*. To love God's works rather than God himself is "the origin of all impiety," he argues. Having thus identified sin with idolatry, Augustine immediately sketches out the idolatrous options open to people as they choose to worship some aspect of creaturely reality: some worship the rational soul, others the human person as such; still others "slip further down and worship animals and even material things"; and there are those who "think themselves most religious who worship the whole created universe," which "they think to be one great God, of whom all things are parts."[4] Augustine could easily have expanded his list of possibilities to include other creaturely objects of loyalty and reverence: nations, ethnic identities, profit, power, and pleasure.

Augustine's account here focuses primarily on the affective dimensions of unbelief: he is interested in the fact that diverse idolatries are grounded in different creaturely "loves." But this account can also be applied to the way in which people *think* about reality, to the ways in which nontheocentric intellectual perspectives are based upon a selective response to the manifold works of the Lord.

On this analysis, creature-centered thought is reductionistic in character: people will organize their understanding of reality around an "absolutizing" of some aspect of the creaturely. But they do have a variety of options available to them as they attempt to expedite their reductionistic projects. When we fail to orient our thinking toward the reality of God, we have many aspects of creaturely existence to choose from in relocating our "ultimate" reference point.

4. St. Augustine, *Of True Religion*, trans. J. H. S. Burleigh, with an Introduction by Louis O. Mink, Gateway Edition (Chicago: Henry Regnery Co., 1959), 65-66.

We should expect non-Christian thought, then, to exhibit a pluriform pattern. And this expectation is borne out by intellectual realities. For the Freudian, the basic categories are psycho-biotic ones — so that even belief in God itself is accounted for in terms of these categories. For the Marxist, reality is interpreted in political-economic terms, for the Nietzschean, human creative volition is the organizing reference point, and so on. It is not enough, then, to insist that non-Christians will inevitably view reality differently than Christians do. It is also important to acknowledge the likelihood that non-Christians themselves will disagree with each other in choosing the appropriate reference points and categories. The fact that God's works are manifold has implications for the way people behave intellectually when they insist on denying God's reality.

Non-Christian thinkers have themselves become very sensitive in recent decades to the potential for extensive directional diversity. Indeed, this kind of meta-awareness of the seemingly endless possibilities for deep and incommensurable directional differences is, as we shall see shortly, often set forth as a defining feature of the contemporary consciousness. In such a context it is especially important for Christians to probe the patterns of directional pluralism. As we address this topic in the rest of this chapter, we will assess two contemporary meta-accounts of directional pluralism: the "post-modern" perspective, which has a rather relativistic, even skeptical, flavor; and the dialectical overview that has been proposed as an alternative to relativism/skepticism by several contemporary thinkers, including some Christian theologians.

"POSTMODERN" PLURALISM

Many analysts of the "postmodern" consciousness are convinced that the contemporary form of "the problem of pluralism" has some novel aspects to it. The human cognitive quest, they argue, has become permanently fragmented into multiple discourses. No binding "meta-narrative" is available to unify these diverse conversations; indeed, the unifying visions that guided our lives in the past were instruments used by the powerful classes to impose their wills upon the whole. "We have paid a high enough price for the nostalgia of the whole and the one," says Jean-Francois Lyotard; the time has come to "wage a war on totality" by becoming "witnesses to the unpresentable."[5]

It is not enough simply to dismiss this kind of skepticism as yet another appearance in the ongoing historical parade of relativisms. As Peter Berger has observed, our contemporary awareness of directional plurality as a boundless manifold is grounded in experiences of radical social change unique to our historical era. "Modernity," he argues, is characterized by a "near-inconceivable expansion of the area of human life open to choices," producing an "emporium of life-styles, identities, and religious preferences."[6]

The skeptical mood is grounded, then, in the experience of very real social conditions. But it is not clear that the "postmodern" celebrants are actually operating in a consistently skeptical manner. Quentin Skinner makes this point in explaining why he has chosen to treat the perspectives of such thinkers as Foucault, Wittgenstein, Feyerabend, and Derrida as examples of "contributions to a return of Grand Theory in the human sciences":

[T]he joke, so to speak, is on the sceptics themselves. Although they have given reasons for repudiating the activity

5. Jean-Francois Lyotard, *The Postmodern Condition: A Report on Knowledge,* trans. Geoff Bennington and Brian Massumi, Foreword by Frederic Jameson, Theory and History of Literature, vol. 10 (Minneapolis: University of Minnesota Press, 1984), 81-82.
6. Peter Berger, *The Heretical Imperative,* 3, 27.

92

of theorizing, they have of course been engaged in theorizing at the same time. There is no denying that Foucault has articulated a general view about the nature of knowledge, that Wittgenstein presents us with an abstract account of meaning and understanding, that Feyerabend has preferred an almost Popperian method of judging scientific hypotheses, and even Derrida presupposes the possibility of constructing interpretations when he tells us that our next task should be that of deconstructing them. . . . [A]lmost in spite of themselves, they have proved to be among the grandest theorists of current practice throughout a wide range of the social disciplines.[7]

Skinner's comments provide a graphic explication of some observations that we made in our first chapter: that insoluble problems arise when directional pluralism is taken as the final horizon, and that not every position initially appearing to be an ultimate pluralism turns out to be one upon careful examination. Having underscored these contentions, we will now attempt to articulate a plausible alternative to postmodern skepticism.

A FALSE CHOICE

Richard Bernstein has argued that our contemporary discussions of seemingly basic pluralities are often characterized by an unfortunate tendency to formulate the alternatives in strictly bipolar terms. People seem to think that they must choose between "objectivism" and "relativism." We must examine Bernstein's insistence that this is a false choice as we consider the options available for a Christian perspective on these matters.

---

7. Quentin Skinner, ed., *The Return of Grand Theory in the Human Sciences* (Cambridge: Cambridge University Press, 1985), 12-13.

"Objectivism" in Bernstein's scheme is "the basic conviction that there is or must be some permanent, ahistorical matrix or framework to which we can ultimately appeal in determining the nature of rationality, knowledge, truth, reality, goodness, or rightness." In contrast, "relativism" is the denial that such a matrix exists, the insistence that any notion of rationality, knowledge, truth, reality, goodness, or rightness we might employ in deciding between competing claims must "in the final analysis" be seen as itself "relative to a specific conceptual scheme, theoretical framework, paradigm, form of life, society or culture."[8]

Here we have what looks like a fairly basic and unavoidable choice. When confronted with two rather general and incompatible conceptual schemes, either there is a more general or ultimate standard by which we can judge the more reasonable or adequate scheme, or there is not. It may seem a bit odd, then, that Bernstein would look for an alternative that is "beyond objectivism and relativism." On closer examination, however, it is clear how such an alternative is possible. He introduces into his account of objectivism the requirement that the more general or ultimate reference point be embedded in "some permanent, ahistorical matrix or framework." This allows him to search for a point of view that is less "permanent" and "ahistorical" than the objectivist account he has delineated, and yet avoids relativism by appealing to norms that are themselves historically embedded.

In an earlier discussion in his *The Restructuring of Social and Political Theory*, Bernstein concludes his sympathetic examination of seemingly disparate strands in social-political theory with an expression of Hegelian hope:

[A]s Hegel has taught us, the history of culture develops by the assertion and pursuit of what appear to be irreconcilable

8. Bernstein, *Beyond Objectivism and Relativism*, 8.

conflicts and oppositions. We can discern in these "moments" a pattern that reveals how we grasp both their "truth" and their "falsity." As we work through these moments, we learn how what is true in each of them can be integrated into a more comprehensive understanding that enables us to reject what is false, partial, one-sided, and abstract.[9]

This serves as a concise account of the position that Bernstein defends at greater length in *Beyond Objectivism and Relativism*. In this later work he continues to be optimistic about the ways in which diverse philosophical perspectives might point the way to a more comprehensive vision of the future. Not that Bernstein is willing to commit himself to firm predictions about the outcome of the historical process. But as is clear from the concluding thought in these cautious comments, he does not doubt that the real possibility of a future consensus is anchored in our very nature as human beings:

> There is no guarantee, there is no necessity, no "logic of history" that must inevitably lead to dialogical communities that embrace all of humanity and in which reciprocal judgment, practical discourse, and rational persuasion flourish. If anything, we have or should have learned how much the contemporary world conspires against it and undermines it. And yet it is still a *telos,* a *telos* deeply rooted in our human project.[10]

9. Richard J. Bernstein, *The Restructuring of Social and Political Theory* (Philadelphia: University of Pennsylvania Press, 1978), 235.
10. Ibid., 231.

CHRISTIAN DIALECTICISM?

It might seem obvious to some that Christianity, at least on any orthodox reading of Christian teaching, is a straightforward objectivism as Bernstein lays out the objectivist perspective. If God is unchanging, and if all questions about reality, knowledge, and value are ultimately decidable from the divine point of view, then it is difficult to see how Christians can avoid subscribing to some form of objectivism.

To argue along these lines seems quite legitimate. Still, some nuances need to be introduced. And one way of addressing them is to think about why some Christians might share Bernstein's interest in finding an alternative to both objectivism and relativism.

Bernstein's dialectical approach attempts to avoid relativism not by positing some sort of "ahistorical matrix," but by working toward a consensus that must itself be arrived at by means of a historical process. There are thinkers in the Christian community who express a similar hope for a dialectically produced synthesis. To cite one prominent case: in his book *God Has Many Names,* John Hick expresses the confident expectation that we will someday achieve not merely a synthetic Christian theology, but an even broader "world theology":

> [Such] a global theology would consist of theories or hypotheses designed to interpret the religious experience of mankind, as it occurs not only within Christianity, but also within the other great streams of religious life, and indeed in the great non-religious faiths also, Marxism and Maoism and perhaps — according to one's definition of "religion" — Confucianism and certain forms of Buddhism. The project of a global theology is obviously vast, requiring the co-

operative labours of many individuals and groups over a period of several generations.[11]

Hick's way of sketching out his dialectical scenario relies heavily on a scientific-testing kind of imagery: through "the co-operative labours of many," different religious and quasi-religious movements work toward a consensus by presenting "theories or hypotheses" for dialogic examination. Paul F. Knitter, who also looks for a historically produced consensus theology, articulates a vision that relies more explicitly on the view of history associated with "a kind of Teilhardian religious evolution." The world religions, Knitter contends, are presently "evolving out of the *micro phase* of religious history in which the various traditions grew and consolidated in relative isolation from each other . . . toward a *macro phase* of history in which each religion will be able to grow and understand itself only through interrelating with other religions."[12]

Knitter's dialectical process is much less "intellectual" than the development described by Hick. For one thing, it is undergirded by a much stronger and more explicit account of the direction of history; the interaction among religions is purposefully borne along by the historical flow. But the requisite elitist dialogue also involves much more than the presenting of Hick's "theories or hypotheses." In Teilhardian fashion, Knitter envisions a new breed of theologian who will be able to take on not just more facts about other religions, but the kind of "new consciousness" that "nurtures the creeds and codes and cults of other religions."[13]

11. John Hick, *God Has Many Names: Britain's New Religious Pluralism* (London: Macmillan, 1980), 8.
12. Paul F. Knitter, *No Other Name? A Critical Survey of Christian Attitudes Toward the World Religions* (Maryknoll, N.Y.: Orbis Books, 1985), 225.
13. Ibid., 226.

THE LIBERATIONIST DIALECTIC

For the purposes of clarifying the relevance of Bernstein's typology for Christian thought, it is helpful to see how the Hick-Knitter dialectical perspective differs from that of liberation theology. Actually, liberation thought can rather easily be classified as objectivist in Bernstein's scheme.

This will seem surprising to some. After all, aren't many liberation theologians influenced, often by their own admission, by Marxist categories? And is not Marxism a perspective in which "dialectic" and "synthesis" have a prominent place?

The answers to both of these questions is affirmative — in a sense. Liberation thinkers have certainly made use of eschatological notions, arguing that God is at work in the present age, preparing the world for a new and exciting future in which a very different societal order will obtain. And they believe that "the poor and the oppressed" are in an important sense the vanguard of this new world order.

This way of making the case has, in turn, some obvious parallels to the Marxist scheme, in which the proletariat is viewed as the "universal class" whose groanings and yearnings are in fact shaped by desires that point proleptically to the post-revolutionary age. And many Christian proponents of liberation theology have been directly influenced by Marxism in spelling out their understanding of the special eschatological status of "the poor and the oppressed." Yet the notion that the politically and economically marginalized have a special kind of eschatological status in the biblical scheme is something that can be defended quite apart from any reliance on Marxist support. The Bible does make it clear, after all, that there is an important sense in which the poor are "blessed," and that those who hope to participate in the joys of the future Kingdom must cast their lot with those who suffer in the present age.

In any event, it is precisely this emphasis on the special

eschatological status of "the poor and the oppressed" that distinguishes the view of most liberationists from the vision of Hick and Knitter. For liberation thinkers, we can already discern much of what the final "synthesis" will look like, since the yearnings and groanings of the oppressed of the present age are signposts and pointers to the ultimate purposes toward which God is directing history. The theological hope of the oppressed is not merely one among many diverse elements that will ultimately be drawn together in a final global theology. That ultimate theology must conform to standards and norms that are already available to us — the patterns that emerge out of present-day reflection on the meaning of oppression.

The "wait-and-see" character of Hick's and Knitter's speculations about the final shape of global theology is, then, not at all typical of liberationism. Their expectations regarding the coming historical consensus are much more open-ended about the shape of the future than the liberationist scheme permits. Hick and Knitter believe that the norms for decisively assessing present-day theologies will eventually become clear. But we do not, in their account, *presently* possess those norms. At best we must operate with a sensitivity to what will or will not move us creatively in the direction of newness for the future. And that sensitivity, while not very precise, will surely manifest a discernible bias in favor of generality, inclusiveness, and an open-ended spirit; a willingness to think new thoughts and "pass over" into new experiences.

HISTORICAL EMBEDDEDNESS

When Bernstein delineated the objectivist perspective so that the idea of a "permanent ahistorical matrix" for determining truth was a crucial feature, he was signalling a very important issue. Both relativism and the Bernstein-Hick-Knitter brand of dialecticism take historical processes very seriously — to the point that they can be characterized as strongly "historicist." Relativism assumes that the plurality of historically developed perspectives is a "given" that we cannot get beyond. Dialecticism, on the other hand, does look for norms that will help us adjudicate between incommensurate claims and visions. But these norms, which will eventually provide the reference point from which the adequacies and inadequacies of various historical particularities can be judged, will themselves emerge out of the historical interaction among those existing particularities.

Still, some Christians will not be satisfied with any position that fails to appeal to some sort of "permanent ahistorical matrix" for testing human opinions. For these Christians, then, it is precisely the historicist character of both relativism and dialecticism that accounts for their inadequacies.

This does not mean, however, that we should simply express unbridled enthusiasm for the objectivist perspective. Caution is appropriate, for at least two reasons. First, Christians who consciously identify with an objectivist-type position often tend to confuse the ahistorical with the historical: they treat a viewpoint that is actually closely tied to a historically embedded particularity as if it were *the* "permanent ahistorical matrix" of Bernstein's definition. This is true, for example, of Protestant fundamentalist groups, who often treat a culturally packaged version of "the faith once delivered to the saints" as if it were itself a pure revelation from God. Some versions of liberation theology can also be accused of this tendency, as when a historically particular experience of "oppression" is taken to be the Archimedean point for assessing all other claims to truth.

We do not intend these comments as glib criticisms. We have strong sympathies for the liberationist call for Christians to take seriously the concerns of the oppressed of the earth; and we share fundamentalism's desire to promote the cause of doctrinal orthodoxy. But we also detect in each group a tendency to downplay the cultural limitations of their own perspectives.

In expressing this first concern we suggest that while we take some elements of the objectivist position to be on the right track, we also fear that objectivist pronouncements regularly serve to camouflage claims that do not in fact meet objectivist standards. That is our major apprehension about both liberation theology and fundamentalism: each position regularly fails to live up to its own demands. Secondly, however, we are reluctant to endorse objectivism enthusiastically, because of the way in which such unnuanced objectivism actually nurtures a propensity toward this sort of confusion.

Let us look again at Bernstein's account of the objectivist position: it is, he says, " the basic conviction that there is or must be some permanent, ahistorical matrix or framework to which we can ultimately appeal in determining the nature of rationality, knowledge, truth, reality, goodness, or rightness." If we were forced to formulate our own viewpoint in unnuanced terms, Bernstein's definition here would suffice. But we see genuine dangers in putting the case so simply. In short, we accept his account of objectivism — a position, it must be remembered, that he means to reject — as a minimal formulation of our own position, but we are convinced that real dangers attend this minimal account if it is not expanded and clarified.

DIALOGICAL THEOCENTRISM

The Christian tradition teaches that there is an all-wise and all-knowing divine Person whose perspective on matters of — using the terms that Bernstein lists in his definition — "rationality, knowledge, truth, reality, goodness, or rightness" is indeed the ultimate court of appeal. It is difficult for us to see how orthodox Christians can avoid endorsing some of the elements associated with an objectivist account.

Yet it is not simply our belief in God that *compels* us to look for a nonhistoricist perspective. Our desire for that sort of perspective — one that acknowledges a point of view not affected by the vicissitudes of historical change — is also grounded in a cognitive longing expressed even by people who would not themselves endorse anything like the Christian perspective that we embrace.

It is no accident, for example, that Rousseau in *The Social Contract* regularly resorts to the language of divinity when he describes what it would take for someone to ascertain clearly what the General Will requires.[14] He seems very aware of the fact that his depiction of the General Will promises much more than it can ever deliver by way of concrete human embodiment. Moreover, even our most informed and well-intentioned attempts at consensus can only produce declarations that at best might coincide with the perspective of the General Will in a provisional and approximate manner.

This is not merely a Rousseauean peculiarity. Rousseau is only one important voice in a much larger company that has been looking for a point of view, a perspective, to which — returning again to Bernstein's words — "we can ultimately appeal in determining the nature of rationality, knowledge, truth, reality, goodness, or rightness." Some have, of course, given up on finding such a point of view — thus the relativism that goes back at least as far as the ancient Sophists. Others have insisted that such a point of view is not only available, but that they have it firmly in their possession — thus the pattern associated with the unnuanced versions of objectivism.

14. See, e.g., the opening paragraph of Book Two, Chapter Seven and the concluding paragraph of Book Three, Chapter Four in Rousseau, *The Social Contract,* 41, 75.

The dialecticists rightly refuse to settle for either of these alternatives. They insist that relativists — in so far as there are people who hold to a consistent relativism — give up much too quickly on attempts to get beyond existing stalemates. And yet the dialecticists find it impossible to claim, in the manner of straightforward objectivism, that they themselves have direct access to that standpoint from which all other positions can be weighed and judged in any decisive way. And so they press on in the hope, often buttressed by certain convictions about the way in which history moves, that a human consensus is finally achievable.

An important insight is captured in this dialectist scheme. Yet we believe a similar insight is nurtured in the biblical perspective. We have already noted that for orthodox Christianity the conviction that God is all-wise and all-knowing is nonnegotiable. Closely related to this conviction in the biblical scheme is the claim that the divine Person has revealed truth to human beings: in the Bible, and especially in the incarnate Christ to whom the Bible bears witness.

Does that not mean, then, that Christians must operate with the conviction that they do indeed have clear access to the truth in the manner claimed by straightforward objectivism? In a sense, yes. But alongside this emphasis on the revelation of divine Truth to human beings is another important teaching also very prominent in the biblical scheme: that God graciously creates a community, the church, in which human beings are mandated to work together at discerning God's will, and that this is an ongoing process whose end point will be reached only in the eschaton.

It is interesting that both Hick and Knitter chose titles for their books — *God Has Many Names* and *No Other Name?* — that question a central Christian theme, namely, that the Bible provides us with unique information about God's identity, information that can only be known by God's self-revelation. The New Testament writers tell us to call upon the *name* of Jesus as the one in whom the divine character and purpose have been revealed in a unique and necessary way. This biblical insistence that Jesus alone is Savior and Lord, and that his atoning death and resurrection are crucial to the redemptive transaction whereby human beings are saved from their sins and enlisted for the discipleship that anticipates the renewal of the whole creation — these matters are not open to further negotiation as we move toward a future consensus. Rather, they are the themes that ground and guide our process of discernment.

This way of putting the case, then, differs from dialecticism in that it does not view that human consensus for which we are striving as the ultimate point of view from which everything else will finally be judged. Even the most perfect human consensus must in the final analysis be evaluated in the light of the norms that are possessed and understood fully only by the divine Assessor.

The perspective we are outlining here can be thought of as a *dialogical theocentrism*. Insofar as it does insist upon an ultimate reference point that transcends our human attempts to find consensus, it cannot be satisfied with any form of historicism. But it also takes seriously the need to participate in a community of discernment that is working toward the goal of a consensus that will be pleasing to God when human history is brought to its culmination.

Even though no human consensus is, on this view, a final *producer* of truth, the human dialogic process is still very important — so much so that Christians might well endorse Bernstein's characterization of the human person as especially fitted for "dialogical being-in-the-world."[15] The call to participate in a dialogic community in which people, even people who disagree on important matters, work together to

15. Richard J. Bernstein, "The Rage Against Reason," *Philosophy and Literature* 10, no. 2 (Oct. 1986): 203.

achieve consensus responds to a profound human need as portrayed in the Bible. Human beings are fashioned for covenant partnership with God and with each other; dialogue is a crucial means for facilitating these partnerships.

It is never enough, then, for human beings to claim to possess the truth and simply to proclaim that truth to others. The truths that we are given by God are provided as equipment to strengthen us on a pilgrimage whose distant destination is full maturity. One extremely important way to use that cognitive equipment properly is to engage in dialogue with others who are on the same journey.

THE SCOPE OF THE DIALOGUE

Since we are setting forth this dialogical theocentric perspective as an expression of orthodox Christianity, it is important to take note of the reasons why many orthodox Christians would be somewhat nervous about our use of the dialogue theme. They could correctly observe that we have extended the scope of dialogue beyond the intra-Christian context that has often defined its boundaries. To take the biblical call to participation in a community of discernment as a basis for advocating a broad-ranging dialogue in the larger human community is, they would argue, an illegitimate move. Discernment is a spiritual gift that is given to the church; the dialogic community that the Bible speaks about is not the larger civil society but the *believing* community.

This is a legitimate issue to raise. Many of the biblical passages that one might appeal to in underscoring the desirability of dialogic discernment are ones that deal explicitly with patterns within the Christian community. To apply such themes to a broader community is indeed to argue by extension.

Still, it seems plausible to us to do this. The New Testament writers themselves imply that it is legitimate to extend these intra-Christians patterns to a broader public. We have already noted the call issued in the Epistle to the Hebrews, to "strive at peace with all" (Heb. 12:14). This emphasis is echoed in both the Pauline and Petrine writings: "If possible, so far as it depends upon you, live peaceably with all" (Rom. 12:18); "Honor all human beings" (1 Pet. 2:17). A peaceable "honoring" of people in the larger human community requires an openness to dialogue, especially if the "fruits of the Spirit" — "love, joy, peace, patience, kindness, goodness, faithfulness, gentleness, self-control" (Gal. 5:6) — apply to relationships that extend beyond the church.

This is not to say that dialogue with non-Christians about the basic issues of life is something that will come easily, either for Christians or non-Christians. The Bible clearly portrays the present human dispensation as one in which a basic rupture has occurred within the human race, one that the Christian tradition has regularly depicted in terms of a fundamental opposition between the righteous and the unrighteous. The conflict that this characterization points to is woven into the very scheme of things from the moment of the Fall until the Last Judgment.

To ignore this depiction of human realities is to sacrifice much that is essential to the biblical scenario. Disagreement about fundamental human issues is an inescapable fact of life under present conditions. If there were no other reason for orthodox Christians to endorse some version of pluralism, this alone would be sufficient to cause us to do so. When it comes to the issues of belief and unbelief, the Bible calls our attention to at least one basic plurality: the division within the human community between those who worship the true God and those who persist in their apostasy.

But as we have already noted, no sensitive Christian can be satisfied with a distinction between righteousness and unrighteousness drawn only between communities, with each

106

individual belonging unambiguously on one or the other side of the line. The behavior of "the righteous" is often very disappointing, while "the unrighteous" regularly perform in a manner that is much better than our theology might lead us to expect of them. Thus the need for a perspective that allows for both a rather slow process of sanctification in the Christian life and some sort of divine restraint on the power of sin in the unbelieving community. These theological adjustments to a religious perspective that might otherwise betray strong Manichaean tones provide us with yet another reason for openness to a broad-ranging dialogue: Christians have good grounds for believing that their own weaknesses can be corrected by encountering the strengths of others.

LEARNING FROM IDOLATRIES

What does all of this have to say about the appropriate mode of Christian participation in a broad-ranging civil dialogue?

The Augustinian-type analysis of the diversity of idolatries, presented earlier in this chapter, provides us with some important reasons for Christians to place a high value upon dialogue with non-Christians. The recognition of directional plurality can help us to see the ways in which we can gain new insights from our involvement in a broad-ranging interaction with diverse points of view, even when we consider that diversity to be grounded in idolatrous intellectual projects.

We can draw a parallel in this regard to Paul Tillich's fascinating analysis of neurotic anxiety. The neurotic person is operating, Tillich argues, with a "reduced" sense of selfhood. But this distorted perspective on reality can itself be the occasion for genuine insights. We need not pause to clarify all of Tillich's terminology to grasp the helpful point he is making about the benefits of neurotic selfhood:

Even if pathological anxiety has psychotic traits, creative moments can appear. There are sufficient examples of this fact in the biographies of creative men. And as the example of the demoniacs of the New Testament shows, people far below the average can have flashes of insight which the masses and even the disciples of Jesus do not have: the profound anxiety produced by the presence of Jesus reveals to them in a very early stage of his appearance his messianic character. The history of human culture proves that again and again neurotic anxiety breaks through the walls of ordinary self-affirmation and opens up levels of reality which are normally hidden.[16]

The parallel here to our discussion is that idolatry manifests itself as a substitution phenomenon. Denying the Creator's reality, the unbeliever invests some aspect of the creation with more significance than it deserves. Treating that creaturely element as having ultimate significance, the unbeliever homes in on that dimension of reality with a "neurotic" type intensity. Thus the Marxist's myopic fascination with political economy and the Freudian's with psychic-biotic processes.

Still, this very intensity can yield important insights. The Marxist, for example, can be expected to identify very real political-economic forces at work in familial and religious interactions, influences that others would likely miss. Christians have much to gain, then, from serious dialogue with persons who operate with myopic perspectives.

A similar kind of Christian openness is surely fitting with regard to the more practical dialogues that regularly occur in the public square. There is every reason for Christians to enter wholeheartedly into debates over the laws, policies, practices, and attitudes that are important to public interac-

16. Paul Tillich, *The Courage to Be* (New Haven: Yale University Press, Yale Paperbound, 1959), 66-67.

tion, in the firm confidence that believers can regularly gain new sensitivities from those discussions. Indeed, such dialogues will on occasion force us to acknowledge that we ourselves have been operating with a reduced understanding of the manifold works of the Lord.

CONSENSUS AND DISSENSUS

In emphasizing the importance of dialogue we do not mean to divert attention from the more painful dimensions of directional pluralism. As we have already stated, a theocentric position treats all of our human points of view as ultimately accountable to divine authority. And there can be no escaping the Bible's clear insistence that certain directional perspectives will not be treated kindly in the coming Judgment.

It is a serious mistake, then, to view directional diversity as a mere expression of our rich and colorful human variegatedness. While at least some manifestations of associational and contextual plurality can be viewed in that manner, as we shall see in subsequent chapters, it is dangerous to portray directional diversity in similar terms. Our directional differences come to expression in those very real divisions and conflicts wherein we human persons display our deepest commitments.

There are also more practical reasons why we should not give the impression that directional consensus is a desirable and achievable goal. The downplaying of the reality of directional diversity is regularly linked to official programs that are designed to suppress directional disagreements — the propagation and imposition of civil religions is one obvious case in point in this regard. When this suppression occurs, associational and contextual pluralism will also suffer. Our next two chapters will explore the necessity of promoting these two patterns of pluralism for human flourishing.

⊷ 6 ⊷

Integrative Visions and
Associational Plurality

SINCE IT IS our task in this chapter to examine associational
pluralism, we can begin by asking why the plurality of
associations might be viewed as a subject of concern. The
problematic status of our other two types of pluralism is
easily recognized: directional and cultural diversity are indeed
responsible for many of the difficulties that we experience
in the human community. But why should the fact that people
continue to sustain diverse forms of association — families,
schools, clubs, churches, teams, businesses — be something
to worry about?

The problems related to associational diversity are different
from those of the two other areas. It is appropriate, for
example, to think of conflict as a key feature of both directional
and contextual pluralism: conflict, say, between religious
groups and between ethnic communities. But conflict is not as
important an item to consider in assessing present-day associational diversity. Here the issue is not so much a plurality of
conflicting associations as it is a plurality of spheres of interaction that are *disconnected* from each other.

LOCALIST SOCIAL SCIENCE

We begin with what might seem at first like a detour. We will look at the phenomenon of disconnectedness as it arises not in discussions of associational involvement as such, but in discussions of the *study* of associational involvement. In his discussion of the patterns of 20th-century political thought, Sheldon Wolin offers a trenchant critique of what he views as the fragmented patterns of recent social scientific research. It has been very common in Western thought, Wolin observes, for political thinkers "to identify what is political with what is general to a society," so that "the general responsibility for the welfare of the whole society has been consistently regarded as the special function of the political order."[1] But alongside this tendency, an "anti-political impulse" has also been at work; and it is this latter force that seems to have won out in the last century or so in the study of societal interaction. Scholarly treatments of power and authority have taken on a "localist" texture. The workings of small groups and specific associations and corporations have replaced the *polis* as the most significant area of focus.

Despite Wolin's frequent references to the political, he does not consider this preoccupation with the particular to be peculiar to political science. He insists that the social sciences in general have become increasingly "localist":

> The contemporary social scientist tends to adopt modes of understanding and analysis that are dissective, even scholastic; he is constantly seeking intellectual classifications more manageable than the broadly political one. He is inclined to analyze men in terms of class-orientations, group-orientations, or occupational orientations. But man as member of a general political society is scarcely considered a

1. Wolin, *Politics and Vision*, 429.

111

proper subject for theoretical inquiry, because it is assumed that "local citizenship" — man as trade-unionist, bureaucrat, Rotarian, occupant of a certain income-tax bracket — is the primary or determinant influence on how man will behave as a political citizen.[2]

The pluralistic situation that Wolin depicts is one in which a very fragmented form of associational pluralism has been absorbed into the very study of the plurality of human associations. The "tight little islands" he is referring to are associational entities: businesses, churches, precincts, unions, service clubs. These units have become disconnected from each other in contemporary life, and this lack of connectedness is now reflected, he is insisting, in the very sciences which study that pluriform reality. The difficulties that ordinary human beings have in making connections between their lives as voters and Rotarians and Methodists and parents and sales clerks find a parallel in the difficulties that social scientists have in making connections between the *study* of voting habits and of Rotary Clubs and Methodist congregations and of parenting patterns and of sales forces. Thus we are being offered a form of social scientific analysis in which

cach of us is imprisoned consecutively, so to speak, within a series of disconnected beliefs. None of us is credited with a general set of notions, for we are analytically meaningful only when lodged within certain classifications.[3]

2. Ibid., 430.
3. Ibid.

BEYOND LOCALISM

The authors of *Habits of the Heart* zero in on the same social scientific pattern in their appended essay on methodological issues. They argue that by ignoring the question of an over-arching unity social scientists actually distort their subject matter; for "in the social world, single variables are seldom independent enough to be consistently predictive. It is only in the context of society as a whole, with its possibilities, its limitations, and its aspirations, that particular variables can be understood." Individual social facts can be properly interpreted, then, only with reference to that larger societal whole.[4]

Like Wolin, the Bellah group links this fragmented pattern of social scientific research to a widespread grass-roots experience of social fragmentation. Bellah and his colleagues argue — and the influence of Alasdair MacIntyre's *After Virtue* is obvious here — that "the culture of manager and therapist" both reflects and reinforces the fragmenting of life that comes with radical role segmentation, as managerial and therapeutic techniques devote themselves to making "our particular segment of life a small world of its own."[5]

In raising these issues, the Bellah team and Wolin are expressing a concern for the health of society as such. Human communities cannot long tolerate role-fragmentation. Either a society will achieve unity by recovering an integrative vision or — and this is a danger which both Wolin and the Bellah group explicitly point to — the unity will be imposed on the society by totalitarian means.

Both Wolin and the Bellah team insist that the solution to this fragmentation must come in the form of an integrative vision. Moreover, the integrative vision they call for as a

4. Bellah, *Habits of the Heart,* 300.
5. Ibid., 50.

corrective for *associational* fragmentation is a perspective that is unmistakably *directional* in nature. Indeed, their proposed cures for associational segmentation make much of the need for directional integration. In both discussions the solution to the problems associated with both role diversity and role-study diversity must be found in a connected vision of what the good life is for people in their social humanness.

Wolin offers three suggestions of how the requisite connecting vision can be covered in modern society: first, we have to find ways in which the citizen-role generates the kind of "integrative experience" that ties other roles together; second, "the political art" must once again be a means of striving for the kind of "integrative form of direction . . . that is broader than that supplied by any group or organization"; and third, political theorists must once again wrestle "with what is general and integrative to men, a life of common involvements."[6]

There is no reason to think that Wolin's call for more attention to the "general" and the "common" is intended as a substitute for associational pluralism as such. Indeed, he seems to share the Bellah group's conviction that a lively and healthy associational diversity is an important and necessary means for promoting a more integrated political order. Nor are Wolin and the Bellah group calling for an integrating vision that will somehow be enshrined in the public square. They are not insisting that a social order cannot survive without some official or quasi-official public philosophy. Rather, they are suggesting that for the health of society it is important for people to be thinking about how to integrate perspectives, and how to advocate on behalf of their preferred visions in a broad-ranging public dialogue.

6. Wolin, *Politics and Vision,* 434.

BOUNDED SELFHOOD

The call for healthier patterns of associational diversity is echoed by psychologist Martin Seligman in an article on the rising rates of clinical depression among North American "baby boomers" in the 1980s. Seligman insists that contemporary culture has produced a very unhealthy kind of self, one "whose pleasures and pains, whose successes and failures occupy center stage in our society."[7] He further argues that this self-centeredness is closely related to a widespread confusion about the proper boundaries of our selfhood.

Seligman observes that we moderns are encouraged to set very ambitious goals for our lives. When the inevitable disappointments set in, we lack social support systems to fall back upon. When personal setbacks occurred in the past, we could regularly rely on "larger, benevolent institutions (God, nation, family)" that would "help us cope with personal loss and give us a framework for hope. Without faith in these institutions, we interpret personal failures as catastrophic." Our only hope, says Seligman, is to "scale down our preoccupation with comfort and discomfort and make a renewed commitment to the common good."[8]

Seligman's probings comport well with the views of certain recent social commentators who have been emphasizing the importance of strong "mediating structures" such as families, churches, synagogues, ethnic alliances, and a variety of community and service organizations for providing people with a sense of bounded identity. This is obviously a viewpoint endorsed by the Bellah team, MacIntyre, and Wolin — although we will refer shortly to some writers who have made the case in much more detail.

7. Martin E. P. Seligman, "Boomer Blues," *Psychology Today* 22, no. 10 (Oct. 1988): 52.
8. Ibid., 55.

The defense of mediating structures highlights the way in which diverse associations provide a buffer zone that can help us to avoid, for example, the false choice between individualism and statism in political life. It is not the case that the only way for persons to avoid being absorbed into state-defined roles is to promote a sense of radical individuality. An alternative is to promote and strengthen societal structures — churches, families, and the like — that will provide a non-statist sense of communal identity.

Seligman extends this argument into the more intimate realm of the psyche. People need boundaries in order to maintain a sense of identity. Mediating structures provide us with the roles and allegiances that can prevent us from narcissism on the one hand and totalitarianism on the other.

THE RELEVANCE OF THE DIRECTIONAL

Peter Berger has devoted considerable attention to the role of mediating structures. He seems to have associational diversity in mind when he describes his own perspective as one that "respects the pluralism of American life."[9] The "megastructures" of human interaction, on Berger's analysis, cannot provide for their own health without help from elsewhere. States and corporations need to draw their "moral sustenance" from "below" themselves.[10] These associations that stand between the individual and the larger mega-entities are the embodiments of "the living subcultures from which people derive meaning and identity."[11] It is of the utmost importance to respect their mediating role.

9. Peter Berger, "In Praise of Particularity: The Concept of Mediating Structures," in his *Facing Up to Modernity: Excursions in Society, Politics, and Religion* (New York: Basic Books, 1977), 140.
10. Ibid., 134.
11. Ibid., 139.

The defense of mediating structures is both timely and sensible. But it is also important to be clear that this endorsement of associational pluralism is closely linked to an appreciation for directional pluralism. The maintenance of a healthy network of mediating structures requires guidance that can only come from directional dialogue.

Directional issues clearly loom large in the cases set forth by the Bellah team and Wolin. They do not advocate associational diversity as such. Indeed, the existence of that kind of diversity is, on their readings of the situation, the occasion for some of the most serious problems of contemporary life. People are experiencing radical role-fragmentation. Life has become segmented, with no obvious connections between the various spheres of human interaction. And this radical segmentation has even pervaded the social scientific *study of* those segmented patterns of existence — turning the mental habits of the community of experts into part of the problem rather than a resource for generating solutions.

"DIRECTING" ASSOCIATIONAL DIVERSITY

To repeat: Wolin and the Bellah group are not objecting to associational pluralism as such. In essence their complaint is that present-day associational pluralism has come to be guided by a regrettable directional vision, namely, relativism. The lack of any perceived connectedness among the various associational spheres is due to a relativistic understanding of how those spheres relate to each other.

This is not to say that all the people who are caught up in segmentation, whether direct participants in those associational relationships or the intellectuals who study those patterns of participation, are aware of being relativists. But insofar as they cannot see any connectedness, any unifying visions or trans-associational norms, they are functional relativists.

117

The only alternative to this relativism is a directional vision that will provide the sense of integration that is being called for in the accounts we have been citing. Associational pluralism cannot stand on its own. It will inevitably be handled in the light of some directional perspective.

Yet who will decide which directional perspective will provide the appropriate integrating vision? Two possibilities come immediately to the fore. One is that it will be imposed by some specific group — say, a church or a party or a network of scholars; the other is that it will be generated out of the give-and-take of public debate, without granting any specific directional orientation a favored status in the discussion.

The latter option is, in our view, the preferable one. For one thing, we oppose the imposition of any specific directional vision on the public order prior to the eschaton. This second option, then, is the more *just* arrangement. Wherever possible, people should be permitted to live out the implications of their chosen directional visions. One can cherish such an arrangement without slipping into the relativistic position that all directional visions are equally true; it is not even necessary to hold that every directional vision contains some element of the truth, although that is probably the case. Justice requires that even people whose viewpoints we consider to be blatantly wrongheaded have a *prima facie* right to pursue their sincerely held convictions, provided that they are willing to demonstrate the links between those convictions and the associational patterns they are defending.

From a Christian point of view, we have argued, it is good for human beings to take each other seriously and to explore the actual patterns of agreement and disagreement. From a biblical point of view, we presently live under a dispensation in which it is important to be very conscious of directional differences rather than to disguise them. A society that promotes both associational and directional diversity will not only be acknowledging the minimal demands of justice; it will also be fostering a spiritual climate in which it is at least possible for human beings to live with a self-awareness of the visions that shape and guide their thoughts and actions.

DIRECTIONAL/ASSOCIATIONAL DIALOGUE

Still, we must look a little more closely at the way in which a directional dialogue will provide integrative possibilities for associational pluralism. It is virtually impossible under contemporary conditions to promote dialogue among different directionally committed groups without at the same time promoting associational diversity. In order to see this, we need to be more concrete about the issues that will be addressed in such a dialogue.

The associations we are referring to here are very familiar entities: families, schools, political parties, labor unions, businesses, churches, and so on. A public dialogue about how these various associations should be connected to each other is not likely to occur on an abstract and general level. When the issues of associational connectedness arise, it will undoubtedly be with a focus on questions of specific practice or policy. One common version of the discussion, for example, is in relation to "Who will decide?" arguments.

Take the debate over the permissibility of abortion-on-demand. One legitimate way of construing the controversial issues that arise here is to see them as arguments regarding the proper way of understanding inter-associational relations. Questions about the advisability of having abortions certainly arise for individuals, and often also for families. But they involve decisions on the part of medical professionals as well. Some churches also claim the right to influence decisions and policies in this area. Other voluntary organizations, such as right-to-life and right-to-choose groups, claim a similar right to speak on the topic. Furthermore, schools regularly take it upon themselves to educate students on issues relevant to the topic. And governmental bodies must decide whether and how they are to legislate with regard to such matters.

To decide how to weigh these differing claims and interests requires an integrating vision of how these various associations — individual, family, medical profession, church, school, state — should interact. In the absence of such a vision, the will-to-power will prevail.

What the abortion example also shows, however, is that the directional visions employed in adjudicating these claims and interests will themselves arise out of differing associational contexts. A married couple claims that the right to have an abortion is purely a family decision. A physician insists that she has a right to act in accordance with her informed professional judgment in deciding whether or not to perform an abortion. A church official insists on his duty to address issues of public morality. A feminist organization argues that women have inalienable rights to make reproductive decisions. High school teachers appeal to a pedagogical obligation to train students in responsible sexuality. A political party insists that its party platform will protect us from regressing to the medical dark ages. Such is the stuff of public dialogue regarding integrating visions. And the very diversity of this broad-ranging discussion, with its various directional nuances and themes, is made possible by a rich associational diversity. Debates over directional questions arise, then, not only when churches debate other churches and political parties debate other political parties and activist groups debate other activist groups. They also emerge — indeed, they as frequently emerge — when parties and churches and activist groups debate each other. Associational pluralism contributes in a sense to the vitality of directional pluralism, and vice versa.

120

DEFENDING MEDIATING STRUCTURES

Having argued for a wide-ranging directional dialogue about associational diversity, we must now ask what a Christian perspective can contribute to that dialogue. What sort of integrating vision can Christians provide for a contemporary understanding of associational diversity?

The defense of mediating structures often makes much of the protective and corrective value of associational diversity. We have already featured this line of argument: mediating structures are seen as providing individuals with the buffer zone that will keep them from being absorbed into a totalitarian statism.

This is a legitimate concern from a Christian point of view. Indeed, associational diversity provides people with a kind of protection that extends far beyond the political arena. When people lack the buffer zone provided by a diverse set of associational roles, other sorts of "absorptions" threaten them as well. Popular spiritual monisms, of which the recent "New Age" phenomenon is one (but only one) prominent example, have flourished in Western societies in recent years because dislocated modern individuals — people operating without strong familial, ecclesial, and national bonds — become convinced that their only alternative to an "atomistic" selfism is absorption into an undifferentiated cosmic All. Both spiritual monism and totalitarianism — along with the individualisms that they each oppose — flourish in cultures where little or no buffer zone is provided by mediating structures.

Yet the Christian tradition provides examples of even stronger cases for associational diversity than those that appeal to corrective-protective considerations. Some Christian thinkers have argued that the existence of a plurality of mediating structures has intrinsic value, that associational diversity is in some significant sense an expression

121

of the very nature of things — that it has the kind of fundamental "givenness" that the Bellah team prefers. They have insisted, in short, that God has a strong vested interest in a pluralistic structuring of the patterns of human interaction.

THE TRINITY AND SOCIAL ANALYSIS

One Christian way of providing an ontological grounding of sorts for associational pluralism makes use of trinitarian doctrine. Michael Novak observes that, while St. Patrick saw a metaphorical display of God's triune nature in the shamrock and St. Augustine gave a trinitarian interpretation to the functions of the human soul, he sees the trinitarian formula as having relevance for an understanding of the virtues of democratic capitalism:

> In everything I have been taught to seek God's presence. Thus also in political economy. I find attractive — and resonant with dark illumination — a political economy differentiated and yet one. Each of its component systems has a certain autonomy from the others; each system is interdependent with the others. Each has its distinctive operations, methods, rules. Each tames and corrects and enhances the others.[12]

A more detailed analysis along these lines has been offered by Max Stackhouse, who devotes a lengthy chapter to this topic in his 1972 study of the relationship between theological and sociological thought, suggesting ways in which various trinitarian formulations in the history of Christian thought have had an impact on the understanding of

12. Novak, *Spirit of Democratic Capitalism*, 338.

human societal dynamics.[13] More recently Stackhouse has taken up the argument again, as he examines the thesis — one that he thinks highly plausible — "that inherent in every human civilization is a tendency to plurality, one that requires a certain pluralism of institutional formation."[14] Here is how he appeals to the trinitarian scheme in this connection:

> For those of us who believe that the Trinitarian God is the true God, pluralism is a normative theological belief as well as an ethical or social belief. The metaphysical-moral grounds for dealing with pluralism are at hand. Pluralism within a dynamic unity, understood in terms of persons in community and the community of persons, may be the most important postbiblical contribution of Christian theology to the understanding of both Word and world. It bears on the public life of civilizations precisely because it gives metaphysical-moral articulation to the proper foundations and limits of pluralism. Christians oppose monolithic definitions of ultimate reality, but their pluralistic beliefs are governed by a broader belief in unity. The triune God is integrated. Thus polytheism, the theological form of pluralism without unity, is condemned as strongly as is imperious singleness without differentiation. In using these terms, we see that both pluralism and unity can become blessings or curses, depending on whether our view of pluralism has an ultimate coherence and whether our view of unity has a place for diversity.[15]

While a number of helpful insights are contained in these comments, it is not clear how Stackhouse thinks that the trinitarian scheme actually provides us with "metaphysical-

13. Max L. Stackhouse, *Ethics and the Urban Ethos: An Essay in Social Theory and Theological Reconstruction* (Boston: Beacon Press, 1972), ch. 6.
14. Stackhouse, *Public Theology,* 163.
15. Ibid., 175-176.

moral grounds for dealing with pluralism." He is certainly correct to insist that the God of the Bible is an "integrated" triune being, and that a proper understanding of the divine Trinity rules out views of the deity associated with both polytheism and "imperious singleness." Moreover, one can see how all of this helps to illustrate what a healthy associational pluralism would look like — that, for example, we ought to construe the plurality of mediating structures as a kind of manyness-in-unity.

The difficulty arises when we go beyond seeing the Trinity as a helpful "metaphor" for understanding associational diversity to the thesis that associational pluralism is somehow "grounded" in a view about God's triune nature. Stackhouse thinks that a recognition "that the ultimate One becomes concrete in these three presences demands that we conceive of the one God as becoming operative in human experience in pluralistic ways."[16] But what is the logical force of "demands" here? There does not seem to be any obvious contradiction in the notion, for example, that a triune God whose nature is characterized by manyness-in-unity might actually dislike associational pluralism. Furthermore, what are the proper limits on how we may understand the ways in which God operates pluralistically in human experience? Suppose, for example, that we understood this *à la* Knitter: that the one God comes to have "many names" in the historical process.

This is not to suggest that Stackhouse's proposals here are simply confused. It is likely that a more plausible version of his argument could be constructed. To insist that a belief in a triune God in some sense "demands" a recognition of the need for associational pluralism may be, as we have suggested, to overstate the case. But surely a trinitarian perspective — one that argues, for example, the Cappadocian

16. Stackhouse, *Ethics and the Urban Ethos,* 114.

case for the link between the life of the divine Trinity and human social dynamics[17] — can indeed provide clues that will illuminate the diverse patterns of social interaction. These clues may not be deducible in any straightforward manner from strict trinitarian formulations. But if these formulations can be supplemented by additional data regarding the role of functional and associational diversity in the biblical portrayal of human social reality, then Stackhouse's proposals could gain in plausibility.

CREATIONAL DIVERSITY

A second way in which Christians have attempted to ground associational pluralism in the very nature of things is by insisting that associational diversity has a creational status. The maintenance of diverse patterns of human interaction is intrinsic to the kind of life that God intends for human beings *qua* human beings. Note that this line of argument is not incompatible with the appeal to trinitarian patterns. It could very well be that the fact that human beings flourish best in the midst of associational diversity reflects in a profound sense the very life of the triune Creator. Nonetheless the creational argument focuses directly on the ontological basis for associational pluralism, rather than on themes relating to a doctrine of God.

David Hollenbach sees this creational perspective, which is represented in Roman Catholic appeals to the "subsidiarity" principle, as drawing upon two venerable strains of Christian social thought. From the Augustinian tradition comes the

17. A case for this kind of trinitarian perspective is spelled out nicely by Cornelius Plantinga, Jr. in "The Threeness/Oneness Problem of the Trinity," *Calvin Theological Journal* 23, no. 1 (April 1988): 37-53; see also his "The Perfect Family: Our Model for Life Together is Found in the Father, Son, and Holy Spirit," *Christianity Today* 32, no. 4 (March 4, 1988): 24-27.

insistence that since no single societal institution can fully embody the *summum bonum,* "the pluriformity of human community [must] be respected, and such respect should be institutionalized politically, legally, and economically." And from the Thomist strain comes the teaching

> that these diverse forms of community do not cease to be community because they fall short of the full communion of persons with God and one another that is the kingdom of God. They remain zones where persons achieve their partial but very real fulfillment, a fulfillment that is essentially achieved only in community.[18]

A similar perspective has been set forth in considerable detail by the Dutch neo-Calvinist movement that originated in the late 19th century under the leadership of Abraham Kuyper. The neo-Calvinist argument[19] makes explicit use of creational themes: God built the potential for diverse patterns of human interaction into creation order as such. The original Garden, as depicted in the Genesis saga, is properly thought of as being pregnant with associational plurality. The neo-Calvinists view the Genesis 1:28 command to "fill the earth" as a "cultural mandate."[20] Even if the Fall had not occurred, they argue, a rich associational diversity would have developed as human beings actualized the cultural pluriformity of the creation order. Thus Christians must respect the patterns of "sphere sovereignty."

---

18. Hollenbach, "The Common Good Revisited," 93-94.
19. See Abraham Kuyper, *Lectures on Calvinism,* L. P. Stone Foundation Lectures, 1898 (Grand Rapids, Mich.: Wm. B. Eerdmans Publ. Co., 1931); see also Wolters, *Creation Regained.*
20. For a full treatment of this theme, see Henry R. Van Til, *The Calvinistic Concept of Culture,* Twin Brooks Series (Grand Rapids, Mich.: Baker Book House, 1959).

Herman Bavinck clearly articulated the neo-Calvinist insistence upon the created status of this diversity:

As creatures were given their own peculiar natures along with differences among them, so there are also differences in the laws by which they act and in the relationships which they sustain to each other. They differ in the area of both physical things and psychic things, in the intellectual and ethical realms, in the family and in society, in science and in art, in the domain of earth and in the domain of heaven. It is the providence of God coupled with creation which sustains these diverse structures and leads them to full development. In his providence God does not negate, but respects and unfolds everything which He called into being through creation. Thus He maintains and rules all creatures in harmony with their natures.[21]

While the neo-Calvinists have often gone to great pains to distinguish their "sphere sovereignty" account of associational diversity from Roman Catholicism's "subsidiarity" scheme,[22] those arguments need not detain us here. The two perspectives are grounded in a shared conviction that associational diversity is a crucial element in the Creator's plan for human beings. The plurality of patterns and contexts of human interaction — families, schools, churches, clubs, teams, businesses, guilds — are not important merely as corrective-protective strategies in the face of totalitarian threats.

21. Herman Bavinck, *Gereformeerde Dogmatiek,* vol. 2 (Kampen: Kok, 1928), 571, trans. and quoted in Gordon J. Spykman, "Sphere-Sovereignty in Calvin and the Calvinist Tradition," in *Exploring the Heritage of John Calvin,* ed. David E. Holwerda (Grand Rapids, Mich.: Baker Book House, 1976), 180-181.
22. See, e.g., the case made in this regard by Herman Dooyeweerd, *Roots of Western Culture: Pagan, Secular, and Christian Options,* ed. Mark Vander Vennen and Bernard Zylstra, trans. John Kraay (Toronto: Wedge Publishing Foundation, 1979), especially chs. 5 and 6.

They are fundamental expressions of our created humanness. Both the Thomists and the neo-Calvinists would echo the Bellah group's criticisms of a contractarianism whose associational norms are "subject to incessant renegotiation."[23]

Hollenbach rightly observes that all of our diverse associations fall "short of the full communion of persons with God and one another that is the kingdom of God."[24] This means, as neo-Calvinists have constantly stressed, that our promotion of associational diversity must be guided by the norms of the divine Kingdom. Mediating structures are to be appreciated, not primarily out of a love of diversity as such, but because we honor the purposes of the God who created us in such a way that the maintenance of those structures contributes to our flourishing.

LARGER PICTURES

To bring up the subject of the createdness of societal reality is no minor addition. From a Christian point of view, there is little to be gained from simply pouring our lives into the maintenance of a diversity of mediating structures. It is not diversity as such that human beings should seek to promote. Rather, it is a sense of the unity of a life lived in full awareness of the richness of created existence.

Christianity provides us, then, with an appreciation for associational diversity that is tempered by a vision of the larger unity of the human calling — a vision that reflects, in turn, a sense of the unity of the created order. Christians can enthusiastically support the program of promoting associational diversity. But they will also insist that this endorsement

23. Bellah, *Habits of the Heart,* 140.
24. Hollenbach, "The Common Good Revisited," 93.

must be viewed against the background of a larger account of what human flourishing is all about.

What the Bellah team observed about social scientific methodology applies just as poignantly to the more practical levels of human existence: when we ignore the issues of the overarching unity of human social existence we inevitably distort the particulars of human interaction. It is only when we consider the larger societal picture, "with its possibilities, its limitations, and its aspirations, that particular variables can be understood." To this we need only add that a proper understanding of what our system of human networks as a whole is about will ultimately require that we attend to an even larger picture — because, as Hollenbach has wisely noted, all of our concrete forms of human interaction fall short of the fulness of social existence that is to be found in the Kingdom of God.

⇥ 7 ⇤

Toward the Jeweler's-Eye View

WE BEGAN our first chapter with a reference to an uneasiness detected on the part of social scientists who are confronted with a seemingly unavoidable plurality of paradigms and conceptual frameworks in their disciplines. There is no escaping the impression, however, that for many social scientists this uneasiness borders on disillusionment. As George Marcus and Michael Fischer observe in their recent account of the current situation in social and cultural anthropological research, while earlier anthropology was often pursued with a deep desire to promote the kind of "enlightenment" that can be gained by cross-cultural comparisons, present-day anthropologists have had to abandon the older "hopes for a general science of Man, for discovering social laws in the long evolution of humans toward ever higher standards of rationality."[1] Of course, some anthropologists still nurture more modest and nuanced versions of these hopes; Marcus and Fischer them-

---

1. George E. Marcus and Michael M. J. Fischer, *Anthropology as Cultural Critique: An Experimental Moment in the Human Sciences* (Chicago: University of Chicago Press, 1986), 17.

selves hold out for the real possibility of "the repatriation of anthropology as cultural critique."[2] But they also recognize the strong lure, for some of their colleagues, of a "slide into simple confessionals of field experience, or into atomistic nihilism where it becomes impossible to generalize from a single ethnographer's experience."[3]

The "atomism" to which Marcus and Fischer are referring here is not identical with the "localism" we discussed in the previous chapter. Wolin and the Bellah group were complaining about the ways in which scholars focus on a specific sphere of associational interaction without attending to the larger societal picture. But Marcus and Fischer are worrying about a different sort of myopia, one that limits social scientific discourse to ethnographic reportage: the units here are cultural rather than associational units. The problem Marcus and Fischer describe is not one of concentrating too much on, say, the Rotary Club while ignoring the larger network of associations. Rather, it is one of choosing to speak from within the framework of, for example, a tribe in northern Nigeria without giving thought to the ways in which that cultural outlook fits into a world that is also populated by Koreans, Salvadorans, Austrians, and Scots.

EMPTY SPACE?

The "atoms" of the "atomistic nihilism" that troubles Marcus and Fischer, then, are cultural units. And the "nihil" of the "nihilism" to which they refer is the space that exists between specific cultures: a space that is viewed by many of their colleagues, they fear, as normatively empty — as containing no standards that will permit us to evaluate or compare culturally

2. Ibid., 111.
3. Ibid., 68.

131

embedded experiences. "Atomistic nihilism," then, is a version of cultural relativism: it is impossible, on such a view, to understand a cultural perspective from the outside, and once we move inside we must leave the norms and standards of previous contexts behind us. The successful ethnographer must undergo a kind of radical conversion, with the resulting reportage having the status of a confessional.

In the philosophical literature, the espousal of the cultural relativist perspective is sometimes attributed to Peter Winch, who has done much to place actual anthropological data onto the philosophical agenda. Bernstein points out, though, that the charge of relativism is unfair, as is clear from this comment of Winch's that Bernstein cites, but that is often ignored by other people who discuss Winch's views:

> [W]e should not lose sight of the fact that the idea that men's ideas and beliefs must be checkable by reference to something independent — some reality — is an important one. To abandon it is to plunge straight into an extreme Protagorean relativism, with all the paradoxes that involves. On the other hand great care is certainly necessary in fixing the precise role that this conception of the independently real does play in men's thought.[4]

These comments make it clear that Winch is no relativist. But the concern expressed in the last sentence of this passage has led Winch to put his case in such a way that he has opened himself up to the charge of relativism. Winch goes to great lengths to urge Western scholars to attempt to gain empathy for experiences of social reality that are very different from their own.

---

4. Peter Winch, "Understanding a Primitive Society," in *Rationality,* ed. Bryan R. Wilson, 81. For Bernstein's comments see *Beyond Objectivism and Relativism,* 98.

The well-known Winchian example in this regard is his treatment of Zande witchcraft, a phenomenon that he discusses at length in his essay "Understanding a Primitive Society." Winch resists the unnuanced argument that in their practice of witchcraft the Azande are irrational or less rational than those of us who employ the methods of Western technology. These sorts of assessments betray our unwillingness to consider the possibility that Zande witchcraft may have its own kind of rationality, a variety that is appropriate to its status as a very different practice than the habits associated with our technological manipulation of nature. But can we not say that while Zande magic is a different thing from Western science, Western science is nonetheless a *better* way of manipulating reality or of explaining what happens in the world? This, Winch responds, assumes that we have a right to see our practice and theirs as two ways of doing the same thing — explaining the world, say, or manipulating nature. Here, too, we are importing our standards of rationality, of what it means to explain nature coherently, for example, into the discussion. We refuse thereby to allow the Azande their own ways of making sense of reality, their own patterns of being rational.[5]

While Winch is not a relativist, then, he does take the existence of a plurality of culturally embedded ways of experiencing social reality very seriously. He seems less concerned to combat "atomistic nihilism" — or as he labels it, "Protagorean relativism" — than he is to urge scholars to study with empathy the perspectives of people whose social seeings and doings are much different than those typifying the habits and attitudes of scientific rationality.

5. Winch, "Understanding a Primitive Society," 92-93.

CHRIST AND CULTURE

The Christian community has heard similar calls for an empathic awareness of diverse cultural contexts in recent years. Indeed, it can be said without exaggeration that the past few decades have seen a major reorientation in the ways in which Christian scholars think about cross-cultural issues. The extent of this shift is obvious when we compare the present state of the discussion to the perspective set forth by H. Richard Niebuhr in his 1951 book *Christ and Culture*.

Niebuhr's study has rightly gained the status of a modern Christian classic. Not only has it provided hosts of educated Christians (especially in North America) with the categories in which they think about the patterns of Christian cultural involvement, but it has also had a significant impact on those scholars primarily focussed in the Christian study of cultural phenomena. When we read Niebuhr's book carefully today, however, it seems to be marred by at least one very serious and general defect: an almost complete inattention to the fact of cultural plurality. For many Christians it will now seem an extremely difficult task to spend much time thinking about Christ and *culture* without quickly getting around to questions about Christ and the *cultures*.

For one thing, the intense ecumenical explorations that have occurred since Niebuhr wrote his book make it clear that the differences among the perspectives that he discussed cannot be understood without considerable attention to cultural plurality. What Niebuhr took to be accounts of the relationship between Christ and culture-as-such seem now to be more plausibly viewed as attempts to work out the relationship between Christ and two or more cultural systems. Amish people may be "against" contemporary culture, but not because their Christ stands opposed to culture-as-such; the Amish understand loyal discipleship as requiring them to be loyal to the technological "simplicity" of an earlier rural culture. Roman

134

Catholic liberation theologians undoubtedly believe that Christ is in some sense "above" culture; but this does not deter them from opposing, in the name of Christ, the cultural values associated with the capitalism of the Northern hemisphere. And the "Christianized" culture that is ardently defended in American civil religion is not necessarily the cultural *status quo* — as if Christ were somehow blindly in love with contemporary America; rather, it is an idealized political culture of the past (the "faith of the Founding Fathers").

In short, when we look at actual views and practices of proponents of Niebuhr's typology, we find it difficult to attribute to them a stance toward culture *simpliciter*. Each group is attempting to coordinate the competing cultural claims that are presented to it by what it experiences as rival cultural or subcultural systems.

The situation gets even more complex when we turn from the older ecumenical arguments — Reformed versus Anabaptist, Lutheran versus Catholic — to the newer discussions of cross-cultural matters as they affect the global Christian community. Here the issues raised about "culture" are very different from the ones discussed by Niebuhr. And they raise deep and difficult questions about the cultural implications of Christian discipleship.

These newer discussions have, in effect, introduced a new labelling system into Christian theological discussion. For a long time the most prominent labels used for sorting out Christian theological differences were those referring to various denominational and confessional divisions. Theological positions have been identified as Eastern Orthodox or Roman Catholic or Lutheran or Wesleyan, and the like — along with, where needed, such further qualifying labels as traditionalist, conservative, liberal, progressive, neo-orthodox.

In recent decades, however, a very different set of theological labels has gained some currency. These newer labels divide the theological-confessional landscape with reference to such things as ethnicity, race, gender, and political-economic condition. Thus the emergence in recent years of Black Theology, Feminist Theology, Third World Theology, Liberation Theology and so on. Christians who have begun to take labels of this sort seriously as theological designators argue that much of the so-called confessional theology of the past has been shaped by the cultural agenda, both hidden and not so hidden, of a "North Atlantic" mind-set within which the concerns of people who are on the margins of the white male elitist cultural consciousness are also marginalized theologically.

The defenders of this newer labelling system resist the suggestion that they are the ones who are now introducing cultural factors into theological discussion. The older labels, they argue, are misleading in this respect. The entrenched patterns of dividing up the theological landscape *mask* the cultural factors that have always been at work in theological discussion. On this account, what we have seen emerging in recent years is not "cultural theologies" as such, but rather culturally *self-conscious* theologies whose advocates are now insisting upon more accurate theological labelling.

CULTURE-IN-GENERAL

Niebuhr was not completely unaware in 1951 of issues raised by cross-cultural discussion. But he disposes of the subject rather quickly in a single paragraph in his opening chapter. Noting the argument of some scholars, particularly Troeltsch, that Christian thought and practice have become "inextricably intertwined" with Western culture, Niebuhr confesses his inability to take this charge seriously:

> Troeltsch himself . . . is highly aware of the tension between Christ and Western culture, so that even for the Westerner

Jesus Christ is never merely a member of his cultural society. Furthermore, Christians in the East, and those who are looking forward to the emergence of a new civilization, are concerned not only with the Western Christ but with one who is to be distinguished from Western faith in him and who is relevant to life in other cultures. Hence culture as we are concerned with it is not a particular phenomenon but the general one, though the general thing appears only in particular forms, and though a Christian of the West cannot think about the problem save in Western terms.[6]

This is Niebuhr's stated rationale for his lack of interest in cultural plurality. Since the Christ with whom he is concerned can never rightly be viewed as a member of this or that cultural system, Niebuhr thinks he can legitimately ignore the differences among cultural systems, asking only about how Christ relates to culture-as-such.

Needless to say, this is a bit too facile. Indeed, it has the feel of a *non sequitur.* It is certainly possible to move from similar premises to a very different conclusion. If the Christ with whom we are concerned is never a member of one particular cultural system but "is relevant to life in other cultures," then would it not be important to ask how different enculturations of Christian thought are to be compared and evaluated? Don't we have to ask how Christ *can* be relevant to life in diverse cultural contexts? And since "the general thing" called culture appears, by Niebuhr's own admission, "only in particular forms," must we not then pay much attention to those particularities?

Niebuhr himself gives us the clue as to why he moves so quickly to avoid these issues. He makes it clear in this brief paragraph that his sympathies are with "those who are

6. H. Richard Niebuhr, *Christ and Culture* (New York: Harper and Row, Harper Torchbooks, 1956), 30-31.

looking forward to the emergence of a new civilization," an overarching synthesis-culture toward which human beings of all cultures are moving. He is more interested in "the general thing" than in the "particular forms" of culture, then, because attention to particularities can only impede movement toward the "new civilization."

In a sense it was this very refusal to attend to cultural particularities that accounts for the inadequacy of Niebuhr's analysis of differences among traditional confessional-type groups. We have already noted that very often what Niebuhr saw as a conflict between Christ and culture is better viewed as a conflict between one cultural system, viewed as non-Christian, and another one viewed as Christian. But even that does not yet give enough attention to particularities. Amish communities might appear to be insisting that Christ stands over against all political culture, whether it is the politics of 19th-century rural Prussia or the present-day system of American power and might; but their critique of, say, farming culture or family culture is not nearly so unnuanced. While their Christ may be against guns and voting booths, he is not simply against plows and patriarchy.

In any event, Niebuhr's brief comments on cross-cultural matters exemplify one way in which Christian thinkers have dealt with the fact of cultural plurality: they have assumed that the problems posed by differences among cultural groups are not "deep" issues for Christians to wrestle with. If we focus on culture-as-such, on "the general thing," the surface disparities among various culturally situated understandings of the Christian faith will eventually disappear.

CROSS-CULTURAL SENSITIVITIES

It is not so common these days for Christian scholars, even those with sympathies for the attitudes Niebuhr expressed, to dispose of the difficulties as quickly as Niebuhr did. Most people who think about these matters at all seem to believe that significant attention must be given to issues that arise in cross-cultural dialogue. Many factors can be cited to account for this change of mood since Niebuhr's day. Some of them have to do with the more general intellectual climate — for example, with developments in the social sciences that we have already discussed.

But there are also reasons why the discussion of cross-cultural matters has taken on a special poignancy within the Christian community, particularly among theologians. The close ties that academic theologians have to the Christian churches link theologians with an identifiable international and cross-cultural network of institutions, communities, and individuals — a network that reinforces a concern with cultural differences in a manner not experienced in many other disciplines (with the possible exception, of course, of cultural anthropology).

Cross-cultural discussion, with a special emphasis on the relationship between cultural context and Christian commitment, has been very high on the theological, and broader ecclesiastical, agenda in recent years. And this development cannot be dismissed as a mere passing fad. The focus on these matters has been as intense and sustained among more conservative Christians in the Roman Catholic and evangelical communities, where theological fads are seldom taken as seriously as they are in more "progressive" circles. There is at least one very good reason why attention to these issues has become mandatory for more conservative Christians: Roman Catholics and evangelicals have been in the forefront of missionary activity, continuing to evangelize persons from non-Christian groups long after that ceased to be a high priority activity among mainline Protestants. Consequently, conservative Christian groups are forced to struggle with the issues because of the challenges presented to them by their own converts, who often combine a deep interest in cross-cultural questions with a strong commitment to theological orthodoxy.

These self-consciously Christian discussions of cross-cultural matters have been taking place primarily in environments wherein theologians (especially missiologists) and church leaders conduct their affairs. Not enough attention has been paid to these issues on the part of Christian thinkers who are especially interested in the basic issues of social philosophy. This is regrettable, and our efforts here are an attempt to help correct this pattern of neglect. We are convinced that there is much to draw upon in the existing cross-cultural Christian discussion by which Christian philosophy can be enriched and to which further clarification can be contributed.

CONTEXTUALITY AND LIBERATION

The recent theological attention given to cultural diversity has been associated with two themes in contemporary Christian thought: *contextuality* and *liberation*. In popular discussions — and even sometimes in technical ones — these two themes are viewed as interwoven. But properly understood, they are clearly distinguishable. Indeed, they can actually represent, at certain junctures, opposing patterns of thought, as we will see.

The theme of "contextualization," like its close kin "indigenization," is emphasized by people who want to draw sympathetic attention to the ways in which the Christian message is received, appropriated, and interpreted in diverse cultural situations. These supporters of contextualization urge us to take an honest and critical look, in approaching non-Western or non–North Atlantic cultural situations, at the ways in which presentations of the gospel are often shaped by "Western linear thinking" or "Enlightenment rationalism" or the thought-patterns of "scientific technology." People who issue these pleas for such a closer look favor a plurality of worldviews and, concomitantly, a plurality of philosophical and theological schemes.

Christians who stress "liberation" more than "contextuality," on the other hand, do not necessarily emphasize the importance of pluralism. They will often be quite critical of, say, Third World cultural patterns — even though they may also share the contextualizers' fear of importing the dominant patterns of Western cultural life into other situations.

The different emphases we are pointing to here appear in a published discussion in which the Maryknoll missiologist Sister Joan Chatfield issued an urgent call for the elimination of sexism as it affects both the community of people engaged in evangelizing programs and the patriarchal cultures toward which those efforts are directed.[7] One of the respondents to Chatfield's article, Marguerite Kraft, herself a missionary-anthropologist with much Third World experience, argued that while people in Christian mission have much to learn about healthier gender relations, the sexism issue is

> a western cultural struggle, one which we should not be dumping on the rest of the world. Status and role are given to the individual by the culture and most cultures have a clearly defined division of labor according to the sexes. I do not see this as sexism. There is nobody so blind as one who tries to force her agenda on everyone without first trying to understand from the other person's point of view.[8]

Here we have a clear example of how contextualization and liberation can stand in tension when a specific cultural

7. Joan Chatfield, "Women and Men: Colleagues in Mission," *Gospel in Context* 2, no. 2 (April 1979): 4-14.
8. Marguerite G. Kraft, response to Chatfield, ibid., 20.

141

phenomenon is being assessed. Situations do arise for missiological reflection and decision wherein people must decide whether liberation or contextualization considerations are to be given priority.

The tension we are pointing to here is the same one that Max Stackhouse highlights in a rather sharp manner when he distinguishes between "the new soft, 'pluralistic' contextuality of much current spirituality," which runs the risk of being "the new form of polytheism," and "the hard contextualism of much liberation thought," which can easily function as "the new fundamentalism of the left."[9] To be sure, neither Chatfield nor Kraft fits neatly into Stackhouse's typology as stated; each would insist upon introducing nuances in formulating her position in more detail. Nonetheless, the differing tendencies manifested in their comments point to quite different patterns of thought, a consideration of which raises a very important question for theological and philosophical accountings of cultural plurality: from what point of view, and in the light of what norms, is it permissible to criticize a "contextualized" understanding of the Christian faith?

THE RELATIVIZING TENDENCY

Needless to say, it is difficult to imagine an "anything goes" approach to theological contextualization that still deserves to be called Christian. Not many Christian thinkers would claim the sort of "polytheism" that Stackhouse worries about. When, for example, Marguerite Kraft responded to Joan Chatfield's critique of Third World patriarchy, she did not say that, since right and wrong are culturally relative, sexism should be tolerated in a culture like that of Northern Nigeria.

9. Max L. Stackhouse "Contextualization and Theological Education," *Theological Education* 23, no. 1 (Autumn 1986): 79.

Rather she argued that what might, at first glance, *look* like a Nigerian manifestation of sexism might not actually be so — or might at least not be blatantly so — when the larger cultural context is taken into account. Kraft's argument was not a simple live-and-let-live relativism; instead she was advocating the caution of "first trying to understand from the other person's point of view."

But there are Christian writers willing to concede quite a bit to a relativistic point of view, at least in some of their formulations. We have already looked at an example of this in our first chapter, where we noted Tom Driver's endorsement of a "genuine pluralism of interest, powers, and convictions," as well as his explicit listing of various contextualized theologies in support of his claim.

Another example of a relativistic tendency is the viewpoint set forth by the Asian theologian C. S. Song, who explains the importance of cultural context for theologizing in these terms:

> There is no such thing as a theology immune from cultural and historical influences. Theology is culturally and historically not neutral. A neutral theology is in fact a homeless theology. It does not belong anywhere.[10]

Song goes on to argue that it is wrong to look for an ecumenical theology that is somehow abstracted from, or a "synthesis" out of, particular cultural theologies. The only proper ecumenical theology is, he tells us, one that "is contained within 'particular' theologies."[11]

Song says more than this — and other remarks of his suggest that we should perhaps not put too much weight on

10. C. S. Song, "Open Frontiers of Theology in Asia," *Higher Education and Research in the Netherlands* 26, nos. 3/4 (Summer/Autumn 1982): 52-53.
11. Ibid., p. 54.

these sentences if we are to understand his overall intentions. Nonetheless these comments taken on their own do seem to contain a strong suggestion of relativism. Each theology is tied to its cultural "home." To criticize a properly domesticated theology is to attempt to stand outside of any "home" whatsoever — which according to Song is impossible to do. To attempt such a critical perspective, then, is to smuggle domestic norms from one home to another. All of which seems to suggest that cross-cultural evaluation is simply impossible.

THE ILLUSIVE "CONTEXT"

The notion of a "cultural context" is a rather slippery one and, as Max Stackhouse has observed, the theological literature has seldom addressed the question, "How do we know a context when we see one?"[12] This is obviously not a concern that is peculiar to theological discussion. The problem of clarifying the idea of "context" is no less of a challenge for social scientists. Barbara Frankel's comments on this topic are to the point:

> [T]o speak of context is a peculiarly difficult matter. It is, after all, a slippery concept, for there is no telling a priori where a context begins or ends. Humans live within a set of Chinese boxes, as it were, a social universe composed of contexts of ever-widening extent, from the dyad to the world-system, and from microseconds to millennia. It follows that an indefinite number of bounded contextual units are potentially definable between the poles of the time-space continuum. One problem implied by any contextual approach, then, is to specify for scientific purposes what sort

12. Stackhouse, "Contextualization and Theological Education," 79.

of context we are looking at, so that the universe of discourse is defined in a way making it amenable to critical appraisal by peers.[13]

Harry Kuitert has made a similar case with reference to theological contextualization. How are we to decide, Kuitert asks,

> where the context begins and where it ends, how narrow or how broad it is, in short, what shall serve as a context which provides contextual experience? Is colour of skin a criterion? Or sex? Or are shared collective norms and values? Or ethnic affinity? Must we think of a region? But in that case where does it begin and end? And are all the people who dwell in this region part of it, so that all experience counts, or does only that of some people count? Until there is an answer to these questions the concept of context and therefore of contextual experience is in a void and there is every chance that contextual experience simply means the experience of a group of like-minded people.[14]

Kuitert is asking some very important questions here, but we must be careful to make proper use of his critical probings. Let us follow the lead of his questions with regard to a specific example. Consider the kind of feminist theology associated with a "womanist" perspective, that is, one that insists upon a clear distinction between the ways in which men and women experience spiritual reality.[15] Let us take a

13. Barbara Frankel, "Two Extremes on the Social Science Continuum," in *Metatheory in Social Science,* ed. Fisk and Shweder, 360.

14. Harry M. Kuitert, *Everything is Politics but Politics is not Everything: A Theological Perspective on Faith and Politics* (Grand Rapids, Mich.: Wm. B. Eerdmans Publ. Co., 1986), 70.

15. For a sampling of womanist theological reflection see the Mud Flower Collective's *God's Fierce Whimsy: Christian Feminism and Theological Education* (New York: The Pilgrim Press, 1985).

specific claim that might be set forth from this perspective, namely, the suggestion that the idea of a transcendent patriarchal deity is alien to a genuinely feminine spirituality.

Suppose that a woman with theological training disagrees with this claim, insisting that she possesses a uniquely feminine point of view and that furthermore she finds much spiritual satisfaction in the worship of a God whose nature she understands in transcendent patriarchal terms. Suppose further that her womanist colleagues respond by insisting that she has "internalized a masculine point of view" in doing theology. This kind of response would make it quite clear that the credentials required for formulating a theology based on uniquely feminine sensitivities are not as simple as they initially appeared to be. It is not sufficient, for example, that one be a woman and be a Christian with theological training. These features must be conjoined to some additional criterion, such as the willingness to designate specific spiritual sensitivities as "genuinely feminine."

Similar examples could be cited with reference to, say, Black Theology or Caribbean Theology. Race or place of birth (when conjoined, obviously, to Christian theological training) are not sufficient for membership in the specified community of theological contextualizers. The characteristics designated by the gender or racial or regional labels are implicitly understood to be matched to other features. One must not only be a Christian woman with an interest in theology in order to be a womanist theologian; one must also be aware of certain experiences of oppression related to one's gender, and one must have criteria for linking those experiences to one's theological formulations in a relevant manner.

Again, it is important to treat these critical probings with caution. It would be easy, for example, for our comments here to be construed as an attempt to dismiss contextualization as unimportant for theological understanding. But this is not our intent. The question is not *whether* the oppression of women and North American blacks and Third World peoples is relevant to theological reflection. Such matters are indeed relevant, often centrally so. The question is *how* that crucial relevance is to be formulated. And as Kuitert observes, the connection is not a straightforward one; rather, it "is based on normative ideas about man and woman, white and black, rich and poor and so on. Without these normative ideas there would be no experience of justice, alienation or domination."[16]

The "contexts" featured in contextualized theologies, then, do not generate their own meanings. Gender, race, and region become significant factors for theological reflection only when they satisfy certain *norms* of significance, when we have good reasons for picking them out as important for the ways in which we formulate our understanding of theological issues. It is precisely because they satisfy these norms that the experiences cited by many people who have for so long been "marginalized" in the deliberations of the Christian community can make a legitimate claim to our attention. And it is precisely the existence of such norms that rescues those testimonies from the kind of relativistic atmosphere — the "polytheism" that Stackhouse rightly worries about — that would guarantee their continued marginalization.

OBJECTIVISM AND CONTEXTUALIZATION

Christian liberationist thinkers seldom exhibit tendencies toward cultural relativism. If anything, their views often seem to presuppose an objectivist-type Archimedean point from which they can offer their critiques of specific culturally immersed perspectives.

16. Kuitert, *Everything is Politics,* 72.

For example, the Brazilian liberation theologian Rubem Alves displays objectivist tendencies in his address to the 1979 World Council of Churches' Conference on Faith, Science and the Future. Alves began his response to a British scientist's account of the nature of science with this clever parable:

> Once upon a time a lamb, with a love for objective knowledge, decided to find out the truth about wolves. He had heard so many nasty stories about them. Were they true? He decided to get a first-hand report on the matter. So he wrote a letter to a philosopher-wolf with a simple and direct question: What are wolves? The philosopher-wolf wrote a letter back explaining what wolves were: shapes, sizes, colours, social habits, thought, etc. He thought, however, that it was irrelevant to speak about the wolves' eating habits since these habits, according to his own philosophy, did not belong to the *essence* of wolves. Well, the lamb was so delighted with the letter that he decided to pay a visit to his new friend, the wolf. And only then he learned that wolves are very fond of barbecued lamb.[17]

Alves uses this parable to illustrate his own contention that Western science likes to disguise its own eating habits. Western science, Alves argues, serves the goals of "the scientific civilization" whose ultimate aim is "the final assimilation of all non-western, non-scientific cultures" into itself — thereby dismissing "as superstitious the beliefs of other peoples, considered primitive."[18]

The lambs in his parable, then, are Third World peoples

17. Rubem Alves, "On the Eating Habits of Science: A Response," in *Faith and Science in an Unjust World: Report of the World Council of Churches' Conference on Faith, Science and the Future,* ed. Roger L. Shinn, vol. 1 (Philadelphia: Fortress Press, 1980), 41.
18. Ibid., 42.

as they are immersed in their non-Western cultures, while
the wolves are the representatives of Western Enlightenment
culture. But Alves does not mean to offer a *carte blanche*
endorsement of home-grown Third World patterns, since he
soon applies the lamb-wolf distinction to patterns that occur
within such cultural settings:

> If you ask any dictatorial regime to describe itself, the answer
> will be a marvellous one: nothing more benevolent, nothing
> more democratic, nothing more committed to the welfare
> of the people. But if you go to the jails of political prisoners,
> and ask the same question, the answer will be totally
> different.[19]

No doubt the kinds of dictatorial regimes Alves is alluding
to here often find it beneficial, even necessary, to align
themselves with the forces associated with Western corporate
technology. But Third World dictatorships can be very indigenous: there is something obviously "contextual" about
the regime of, say, a Papa Doc or a Ferdinand Marcos.

Alves clearly has no difficulty finding a point of view
from which he can critically assess indigenous Third World
perspectives. Both the "civilizing" influences from the West
and various non-Western despotic practices are to be rejected
from the perspective of those who are oppressed by these
influences and practices. This perspective is the epistemically
privileged "context" that Alves means to celebrate, one that
is not closely linked to any specific regional or ethnic culture.
The context in question is the experience of a certain kind
of suffering as interpreted in accordance with the categories
of liberation thought.

Once the issues are seen in this light, however, the
differences between Alves and his "civilizing" opponents are

19. Ibid., 43.

not as deep as they might have seemed to be at first glance. As Nicholas Wolterstorff has noted, the "liberation" advocated by proponents of liberation theology is a freedom understood as "self-determination, autonomy, maturation," a freedom for shaping our own destinies as human beings.[20] This is why both Western technology and Third World dictatorships can both be viewed as oppressive. Each represents a force that is taken to be inimical to a certain understanding of "liberation."

The liberationists' understanding of the relationship between norm and context definitely seems to have an objectivist character. They operate with norms that they bring *to* their evaluations of historically shaped contexts. A satisfying cultural context is one that promotes a certain kind of human maturation.

As Wolterstorff rightly observes, not all of the "liberating" impulses that liberation thinkers link to their account of human flourishing are ones that ought to be completely trusted from a Christian point of view.[21] Some of them are sinful impulses, and it is necessary to reflect, in the light of even more ultimate norms, on the ways in which we can discern the genuinely liberating from the pseudo-liberating forces at work in our quests for maturation.

When Christian liberationists are open to this kind of critical review of the Enlightenment account of human flourishing, their perspective approximates the sort of nuanced dialogic objectivism that we are proposing. But when liberationists are unwilling to open their appeals for "liberation" to challenge and review, then their position deserves to be classified as the rather straightforward objectivism that Stackhouse appropriately labels a "fundamentalism of the left."

20. Nicholas Wolterstorff, *Until Justice and Peace Embrace* (Grand Rapids, Mich.: Wm. B. Eerdmans Publ. Co., 1983), 52.
21. Ibid.

CONTEXTS AND ASSOCIATIONAL PRACTICES

We have been taking something for granted in our discussion thus far in this chapter that now needs to be looked at critically. We have assumed that the terms we used earlier to sort out meta-perspectives regarding directional plurality, terms such as "objectivism" and "relativism," can be applied in a similar fashion to contextual plurality. This assumption raises important questions about the relationship between directions and contexts. In what sense is the notion of a cultural context distinct from that of a directional vision? And what role, furthermore, does associational diversity play in a proper understanding of contextual diversity?

It is legitimate to ask whether the idea of a cultural context adds anything of substance to the phenomena we have been discussing prior to this chapter. When some people speak of a plurality of cultural contexts they might actually be thinking of a situation characterized by a diversity of directional perspectives. Thus it might be thought that the difference between Zande witchcraft and a Western techno-logical approach is really a difference of worldviews: the contrast is between the directional perspective of a primal religion and that of Enlightenment thought. If this is how we understand the clash of cultural contexts, then cross-cultural studies provide a very poignant means for considering ques-tions that are fundamentally directional in nature.

An alternative to this analysis would be to argue that the basic differences of cultural context are actually associational in nature. This is one way of construing some comments that MacIntyre makes in a discussion of Winch's views. Very often, MacIntyre observes, the important issues that arise in the study of a culture other than our own are questions about what genres to employ in classifying the activities we are trying to explain. Suppose we are investigating Zande magic; if we ask whether what the Azande are doing is "applied science" or "dramatic activity" or "theology" we may get off to a false start, since "the utterances and practice in question may belong, as it were, to all and to none of the genres that we have in mind."[22]

MacIntyre is observing that sometimes what is taken as a directional difference is actually a difference in activity: it may not be fair simply to classify Zande magic as bad science, because when the Azande engage in their magical activities they are *doing something different* than we are when we engage in scientific-technological enterprise. And one way of looking at these differences is in associational terms.

It could turn out that Zande magic is not correctly identified as technology or drama or religious-cultic practice because it is a different practice altogether; our problems in assessing their magical practices, then, would be like that of the proverbial tribesman who watches a North American football game without being familiar with the enterprise of team sports. Or it could be that the Azande combine familiar associational functions in ways that are unfamiliar to us, producing modes of associational interaction that combine features of what are for us discrete practices into their own unique patterns. This is in effect what the notion of a tribe itself has become for many people in Western culture: the tribal structure combines familiar associational functions — familial, ecclesial, economic, military, etc. — in such a way that the resultant entity seems to be difficult to categorize. If this is what diverse cultural contextual perspectives boil down to, that is, different associational patterns, then cross-cultural study basically turns out to be just another way of exploring associational diversity.

22. Alasdair MacIntyre, "Rationality and the Explanation of Action," in his *Against the Self-Images of the Age: Essays on Ideology and Philosophy* (Notre Dame, Ind.: University of Notre Dame Press, 1978), 252-253.

THE CULTURAL RESIDUE

These are interesting ways of construing contextual differences. But in the final analysis many of us will be reluctant to treat cultural plurality as nothing more than a variation on either directional or associational diversity — or as a variation on a combination of the two.

Trying to eliminate any notion of a cultural residue in such manner is failing to come to grips with the ways in which different cultural groups do in fact combine directional visions and associational practices into unique *configurations* that must be taken seriously in their own right. Take an example already mentioned, the tribe. In one sense we can account for what is "going on" in a specific tribal setting in familiar associational terms. A tribe is a kinship network, a very large extended family, that incorporates into its life associational activities that we Westerners (usually) conduct in non-kinship-based settings: agriculture, buying and selling, military engagement, corporate worship, and so on. Furthermore, *how* a specific tribe understands and gives shape to these activities will depend upon directional factors: what significance they attribute to the cycles of nature, their beliefs about the factors that distinguish them from neighboring tribes, their accounts of how human flourishing fits into the larger cosmic processes, and so on. But the cultural dimension is not simply arrived at by summing up these associational and directional elements. The tribe's "culture" is a way of *patterning* these other factors.

It is precisely the failure to recognize the importance of this cultural patterning as an independent variable that accounts for the superficiality of many Western efforts to "explain" primal practices and perspectives, or male efforts to "explain" the anger of women, or white efforts to "explain" black hurts and frustrations. Such accounts often correctly identify discrete directional and associational factors while

153

completely misunderstanding the larger pattern — the *gestalt* — in which they cohere.

CONTEXTUALITY AND THE *IMAGO DEI*

Herman Bavinck once offered an intriguing suggestion about the nature of the *imago dei*. Most technical discussions of the meaning of the *imago* reference in Genesis 1:26-27 have focussed on the way in which an individual human being might be thought of as being made in the divine image. But Bavinck speculated there might also be a "collective" possession of the image, whereby God in some sense distributes the divine likeness over the human race as a whole. In this sense, only by looking at humankind as a collectivity do we get a full picture of what the human possession of the divine image is all about. Having proposed this notion of a macro-manifestation of the image, Bavinck also suggested that we can think of the variety of cultural groups as having received, as it were, different "assignments" with reference to developing and manifesting those characteristics associated with the divine image. This creational distribution of the image is in Bavinck's thinking, then, a kind of pre-Babel affirmation of the importance of cultural plurality. It is only in the eschatological gathering-in of the peoples of the earth, when many tribes and tongues and nations will be displayed in their "honor and glory" (Rev. 21:26) in the New Jerusalem, that we will see the many-splendored *imago dei* in its fulness.[23]

Bavinck's proposal may be wrong when considered narrowly as an account of what is actually intended by the *imago* reference in Genesis 1. But it is certainly plausible in

---

23. Herman Bavinck, *Gereformeerde Dogmatiek,* vol. 2, 621-622; the relevant passage is translated by Anthony Hoekema, *Created in God's Image* (Grand Rapids: Wm. B. Eerdmans, 1986), 100-101.

its broader intent. To be sure, there is a genuine danger here of reinforcing the kind of racist ideology that finds the "separate development" of ethnic groups to be a showpiece of orthodox theology. In his study of the development of Afrikaner ideology, T. Dunbar Moodie reports that Nic Diederichs, one of the "neo-Fichtean" architects of *apartheid* thought, was fond of insisting that the Creator dislikes "deadly uniformity," which is why, he said, the world contains a plurality of cultural groups.[24] We need offer no reminders of the horrible schemes that have been served by such statements. But those horrors, which ought not in any way to be minimized, often have been justified by the perverse use of arguments that contained important truths. This is the case with Diederichs' observation about what God does to avoid boredom; his claim that God dislikes "deadly uniformity," as it stands, would be seconded not only by Bavinck, but also by many present-day Third World defenders of a variety of contextualized theologies.

CONTEXT AND DIALOGUE

At the very least, Bavinck's proposal illustrates a way in which one can have a deep Christian appreciation for cultural pluralism without being tempted to embrace a thoroughgoing relativism. Marcus and Fischer have suggested that we cannot understand cultural diversity without "a jeweler's-eye view of the world" — a perspective that they see anthropological research as helping us to gain.[25] For Christians, God alone actually has such a view of things, and the adequacy of our human efforts to purchase such a perspective is to be

24. T. Dunbar Moodie, *The Rise of Afrikanerdom: Power, Apartheid, and the Afrikaner Civil Religion* (Berkeley, Calif.: University of California Press, 1975), 156-159.
25. Marcus and Fischer, *Anthropology as Cultural Critique*, 15.

assessed according to the degree we can *approximate* God's "jeweler's-eye view." And these efforts are best pursued by means of dialogue.

The approach we have in mind is nicely exemplified in the views developed by Allan Boesak in his critique of the writings of North American black theologians. Boesak takes note of James Cone's way of insisting — especially in some of his earlier works — that theology must be done "in the light of the black situation." While Boesak has much sympathy for Cone's project, he worries about the way in which Cone formulates the case:

> The black situation is the situation within which reflection and action take place, but it is the Word of God which illuminates the reflection and guides the action. We fear that Cone attaches too much theological import to the black experience and the black situation as if these realities *within themselves* have revelational value on a par with Scripture. God, it seems to us, reveals himself *in* the situation. The black experience provides the framework within which blacks understand the revelation of God in Jesus Christ. No more, no less.[26]

This last comment is a telling one. The black experience, Boesak insists, is not itself divine revelation; rather it is no more than the situation in which blacks have received that revelation. But neither is it *less* than a situation to which God has revealingly spoken. This means that while the black historical experience is not on a par with scriptural revelation, it is at least on a par with *white* historical experience, which must *also* be denied revelatory status.

On this view, cultural particularities are "situations" in

---

26. Allan A. Boesak, *Farewell to Innocence: A Socio-Ethical Study on Black Theology and Power* (Maryknoll, N.Y.: Orbis Books, 1977), 12.

which Christian people receive and give theological shape to the gospel. No such situation constitutes a privileged cultural context as such. The test of theological truth is not whether a claim is espoused by a cultural group in a specific context, but whether that claim can hold up in the light of dialogue that takes place in a posture of accountability to the Scriptures. Divine revelation alone has privileged status as the normative reference point for testing theological claims. And not only for theological matters, but for all of our culturally shaped visions of what makes for human flourishing.

CONTEXTUALIZATION AS META-NORM

Contextual pluralism is *sui generis.* It is not simply a variation on either directional or associational pluralism. Nor is it merely a permissible kind of pluralism to encourage from a Christian point of view. Contextual diversity is an important and positive feature of our created condition.

Indeed, contextualization has a normative status in our understanding of human affairs. More accurately, the need to attend to contextual features is a meta-norm. A judge's verdict in a courtroom proceeding will not be a just one if she fails to attend to the specifics of the situation that she is being asked to adjudicate. Similarly, the more general implementation of norms must itself submit to the meta-norm of contextual sensitivity.

This does not mean, however, that contextual pluralism is the ultimate horizon. The truth or legitimacy of a perspective that is embedded within a given context is not derived from that context. Questions of contextual adequacy must be decided by attending to a more ultimate horizon. Like associational pluralism, contextual pluralism needs directional guidance. In our next and final chapter we will look further at the kind of vision that can generate this guidance.

— 8 —

Under an Open Heaven

W HEN A PROMINENT Israeli rabbi was asked by a reporter about the possibility of finding a biblical basis for a pluralistic solution to Middle East tensions, his answer was not a very hopeful one: "The biblical framework is not the source of tolerance. That's not the place you go to for that. You go there for passion, for zealousness, for extremes. Biblical people are extremists."[1]

While this pessimistic assessment is too unnuanced, it is certainly not a blatant misrepresentation of biblical religion. From a Christian point of view, for example, there is nothing contrived about the problem of coordinating a spirit of toleration with religious conviction. The "ordeal of civility" is no accidental feature of the Christian life. It is a genuine struggle that emerges out of the dynamics of Christian belief and practice.

We do need to be careful, though, about how we characterize the nature of this ordeal. Secularist thinkers are fond

---

1. Rabbi David Hartman, as quoted by David K. Shipler, *Arab and Jew: Wounded Spirits in the Promised Land* (New York: Penguin Books, 1987), 138.

of setting up the discussion in such a way that the burden of proof immediately falls upon Christians to show how maintaining their strongly held religious beliefs is compatible with the appropriate standards of public etiquette. For example, one of the more familiar passages in the Federalist Papers laments the divisiveness caused by "zeal for different opinions concerning religion." The passage goes on to suggest that while the causes of this kind of factional divisiveness cannot be eliminated in our society, we can nurture a form of government that will minimize the effects of such zeal.[2]

Few thinkers, of course, have blamed all of the factional clashes that occur in the civil arena on religious passions. But religious conviction has regularly been viewed as especially resistant to the kinds of accommodations and settlements expected in civil dialogue. Other sorts of factional advocacies are more easily seen as grounded in diverse interests or appetites — which is to say that they are more easily tamed. Religion, however, is a very stubborn phenomenon. Thus Rousseau's insistence, in *The Social Contract,* that "theological intolerance" must inevitably lead to "civil intolerance" — since "[one] cannot live in peace with people one regards as damned."[3] Rousseau wanted to establish the conditions that would provide for a broad public arena devoted to the give-and-take of polite dialogue among mutually respectful citizens — a space that would inevitably become cluttered and restricted, he was convinced, when religious considerations entered the scene. The impression is given, then, that modernity's "civilizing" project creates room for free-flowing public discourse, and that religious dogma only serves to crowd and cramp that public space.

2. *The Federalist Papers,* selected and edited by Roy P. Fairfield (Garden City, N.Y.: Anchor Books, 1961), 18-19.
3. Jean-Jacques Rousseau, *The Social Contract,* trans. Willmoore Kendall (Chicago: Henry Regnery, 1954), 160.

BIBLICAL RESOURCES

There is, however, a more plausible reading of the situation, one in which religious conviction is a part of the solution, rather than simply a major contributor to the problem, of civil intolerance. This alternative analysis has been proposed in a forceful manner in the pages of *Habits of the Heart* and *The Good Society*. The Bellah team is convinced that contemporary society desperately needs the kind of integrative vision that can only be obtained by drawing upon the sensitivities of groups — such as the groups who gather in churches and synagogues — who have maintained their particularized visions of community and belonging and faith in God.

In this regard it is no surprise that the contribution of Alasdair MacIntyre is mentioned at several points by Bellah and his colleagues. In the haunting passage with which MacIntyre concludes the argument of *After Virtue,* he speaks of "the coming ages of barbarism and darkness" that will follow "the new dark ages which are already upon us." If there is hope, MacIntyre insists, it will be realized only through "the construction of new forms of community within which the moral life could be sustained." Thus his wistful sentence: "We are waiting not for a Godot, but for another — doubtless very different — St. Benedict."[4]

There is an important difference on this point, though, between MacIntyre and the Bellah group. Bellah and his colleagues clearly think that nurturing a particularized religious identity can contribute much to the actual restoration of a healthy public space. "[E]xperiences in our own [North American] history," write the Bellah team, "suggest that the churches, synagogues, and other religious associations might be one place open to genuinely new possibilities, where

---

4. Alasdair MacIntyre, *After Virtue: A Study in Moral Theory,* 2d ed. (Notre Dame: University of Notre Dame Press, 1984), 245.

cultivation and generativity have clear priority over exploitation and distraction."[5] But as David Hollenbach has observed, "MacIntyre, at least in *After Virtue,* offers no hope that a larger vision of *public* life can be regained."[6] MacIntyre's call for the formation of pockets of communal-moral clarity in the midst of the surrounding darkness seems to express a mood of sectarian pessimism — a marked contrast to the more optimistic reformist tones of both *Habits of the Heart* and *The Good Society.* Nonetheless, both MacIntyre and the Bellah group share the conviction that it is Enlightenment "civility" and not religiously based visions of human communality that genuinely threatens the social bond. Where they disagree is on the question of whether it is too late to implement the necessary corrective measures. In one sense, of course, only time will tell which of these perspectives is the more accurate one. But if the question is whether particularized communities have the resources to draw upon for working on the project, then the Bellah team seems to be justified in its more hopeful approach.

In their search for antidotes to the pervasive individualism of contemporary life, Bellah and his fellow authors point to a variety of themes that have been employed by Christians in dealing with the foundations of social solidarity. One set of images is based on the kinship motif: for example, "children of God," and "brothers and sisters in Christ." But they note that biblical religion also makes much of "a universal obligation of love and concern for others that could be generalized beyond, and even take precedence over, actual kinship obligations."[7] This understanding of the extra-kinship dimensions of Christian love could be an important reinforcement for civility in public life, since the metaphors that derive

5. Bellah, *The Good Society,* 281.
6. Hollenbach, "The Common Good Revisited," 78.
7. Bellah, *Habits of the Heart,* 114.

from a sense of kinship are not enough to sustain a spirit of civility, which seems to require the utilization of what Sennett refers to as "codes of impersonal meaning."

THE PUBLIC-PRIVATE CONTINUUM

To be sure, Christians ought not to be lured into too strong an endorsement of public impersonality. Sennett's reminder, discussed in Chapter 4, that public selfhood requires a different set of dynamics than do private selves is a crucial one; he is right to insist that our most intimate experiences of interpersonal nurturing do not provide us with adequate codes for our interactions in public space. But sometimes Sennett seems to shift from a rather plausible account of the differences between the more private and the more public patterns of human association to a somewhat more cynical portrayal of the actual contours of social reality. At one point, for example, he suggests that selves that have come to expect trust and warmth and comfort from others are not equipped "to move in a world founded on injustice." Is it not then an exercise in inhumaneness, Sennett asks, "to form soft selves in a hard world?"[8]

For those of us who believe that this world, with all of its injustice and hardness, is nonetheless the creation of a loving God, the contrast between a "soft" private self and a "hard" public identity is not exactly the right distinction. The deep concern that writers like Sennett and Glass show for public selfhood is laudable. But it is important not to posit too rigid a dichotomy between the "public" and the "private." The variety of associational spheres actually exists on a continuum that moves from the more-or-less private to the more-or-less public.

8. Ibid., 260.

The soft intimacy which Sennett takes to be the defining feature of private relationships is not totally out of place in the public domain. Rather than a complete bifurcation let us think in terms of the soft intimacy of our private relationships versus the soft formality of the public square — or a humane and trusting kinship versus the kind of humane and trusting civic affection that cannot rely on those codes and expectations that operate so naturally in families and friendships.

Similarly, the more intimate patterns of human association anticipate something of the formality of the public realm. We have observed in this discussion several writers who have insisted on a very strong contrast between private and public selfhood. As we saw in Chapter 4, for example, Walter Lippmann viewed public life as an arena in which we realize our "second and civilized nature." But this is a misleading way of characterizing the situation. The civil "codes and expectations" that Sennett and Lippmann take to be so crucial to the maintenance of public selfhood do not simply *originate* in the public arena. They are already present in rudimentary forms in the softer spheres of human interaction. There is a common good that must be respected in both families and therapy groups. Children and spouses have the right not to be abused in the privacy of the nursery or the bedroom. And the patterns of civility are often as important to respect at the family dinner table as they are in the legislative assembly.

This is not a small quibble. Lippmann's language (our "second and civilized nature") easily lends itself to the notion that it is the function of public life, and more specifically the task of the state, to transform us into more "human" beings by rescuing us from our more instinctual and "hidden" (Arendt's term) selves. This gives much more responsibility to public institutions than they need, or have a right, to carry. Public interaction does not make us over, giving us a brand new nature. Rather it facilitates the further unfolding, the

163

opening up, of that which is already present in other spheres of interaction. And the political corollary of this emphasis should be obvious: if the work of the state reinforces and builds upon that which has already occurred in the less public associational contexts, then the state must respect and protect those more intimate spheres as having their own integrity within the civilizing scheme of things.

WORSHIP AND PUBLIC CONSCIOUSNESS

When a rigid distinction is maintained between public and private, it is difficult to see how the strengthening of associational diversity can contribute anything to the maintenance of a healthy public arena. But when the continuities between the less-public and the more-public spheres of interaction are recognized, it is easier to appreciate the contributions that various associational contexts can make to the formation of public selfhood. Rousseau seemed to have some sense of the significance of these continuities. No philosopher has struggled more intensely with the problem of public selfhood than he did, and in one sense he presupposed a rather stark contrast between public and private. Our natural human impulses, as Rousseau viewed things, do not make the consciousness that is necessary for citizenship an easy thing to attain. In the best-known passages of *The Social Contract* dealing with this subject, Rousseau insists that the transition from the state of nature into the cooperative social bond requires a radical transformation of the ways in which we experience inter-psychic reality.

Still that is, for Rousseau, merely to state the problem. The question that vexed him — and which he explored throughout many of his writings — was how this transformation could take place. In his most hopeful proposals he envisioned public consciousness as a kind of expansion of the more "natural" experiences of familial and tribal kinship, which he imagined as occurring in those public moments when people are suddenly awash in the psychic overflow that results from an expanded sense of selfhood. At one point, for example, Rousseau thinks about the way in which the experience of citizenship might spring up in the course of a communal festival when, energized by warm sunshine and gentle breezes, the participants "become an entertainment to themselves," so that "each one sees and loves himself in the others, and all will be better united."[9] And in another place he speaks of the experience of a "patriotic drunkenness . . . which alone can raise men above themselves."[10]

It should not surprise us that a pagan thinker like Rousseau would gravitate toward images of summer picnics and drunken parties as he tries to imagine how a civilizing self-transcendence might be attained. But in searching for mechanisms that make use of the festive and the celebrative, Rousseau seems to be pointing in his own way to a link between public consciousness and the sense of mystery that Christians associate with the worship experience.

The Bellah team are very explicit about this kind of link in their own account of what goes into a healthy public selfhood. They suggest that perhaps "the most important thing of all" in our attempts to find communal commitment and civic friendship is "common worship, in which we express our gratitude and wonder in the face of the mystery of being itself."[11] And Richard Bernstein explores a similar theme when he tells us that a civil rights gathering held in a Baptist church in Mississippi "was one of the most impressive political gatherings I have ever attended" precisely be-

9. Rousseau, Letter to d'Alembert, quoted by Marshal Berman, *The Politics of Authenticity: Radical Individualism and the Emergence of Modern Society* (New York: Atheneum, 1970), 215.

10. Ibid., 283.

11. Bellah, *Habits of the Heart,* 295.

cause it "had something of the quality of a religious meeting" — thus creating a context, he testifies, in which "I was witnessing the creation of just one of those public spaces that Arendt describes."[12]

FINDING A BASIS FOR UNITY

Rousseau's call for a community festival is further evidence that the public square can never remain "naked." Rousseau wants to ban Christianity because it is too divisive; but as he makes clear in his well-known passage on civil religion, he immediately substitutes a new religion.[13] His proposed civil religion will have no creeds, but it will require an act of regeneration, a "radical transformation." Another striking example is provided by Auguste Comte, whose austere defense of positivism ended with a program for the worship of humanity itself as the Great Being.

These examples lead us to the conclusion that social unity cannot be conceived of in a thoroughly immanentistic manner. This contention is reinforced by Jürgen Habermas's discussion of these topics. To many observers, Habermas's thought epitomizes the contemporary *post-religious* understanding of society. But on closer scrutiny it becomes clear that Habermas himself can only develop his communication theme by introducing religiously laden metaphors, such as "covenant" and "atonement."[14] One does not find here Rousseau's civil religion, nor Comte's cult of "Mankind"; rather, Habermas's concern is to demonstrate the need for, as well as the possibility

---

12. Richard J. Bernstein, "The Meaning of Public Life," in *Religion and American Public Life: Interpretations and Explorations*, ed. Robin W. Lovin (New York: Paulist Press, 1986), 48.

13. Rousseau, *The Social Contract*, 158-162.

14. See Sander Griffioen, "The Metaphor of the Covenant in Habermas," *Faith and Philosophy*, vol. 8 (October 1991), 524.

of, a basic solidarity that would exclude neither differences nor conflicts. It is significant that even Habermas is not able to discuss such matters without using religious language.

To be sure, thinkers like Rousseau and Habermas continue to envision society as constituting its own ultimate horizon. At best, then, their affirmations of human self-transcendence are from a biblical point of view distortions of the truth. Unity under these conditions cannot help but be detrimental to diversity, for if it is sought within the horizon of created reality, intolerance is bound to emerge at one point or another. Remember the Rousseauean warning that some citizens would need to be "forced to be free"; and those who would not submit to this coerced liberation were placed "outside of nature," as in the case of poor King Louis XVI.[15] Comte also echoes this theme. His "religion of altruism" had no place for those allied with the Reformation, a movement that he considered to be the source of contemporary anarchism.[16]

Even Habermas's idea of communication is less universalist than it purports to be. While Habermas insists that the only way nowadays to conceive of the Enlightenment idea is as a universal covenant that would "potentially" include those who oppose its very principles, he in fact excludes from universal communication — that is, he *excommunicates* — certain groups of people, such as Nazi criminals and those contemporary German historians who have attempted to develop an apologetic for the Third Reich.[17]

15. "To set yourself outside the nation, and in opposition to the general will was to put yourself outside nature itself. Saint Just and Robespierre deemed that Louis Capet (ci devant Louis XVI) was hors nature, a monster; so that cutting off his head did not even amount to manslaughter": Conor Cruise O'Brien, "The Decline and Fall of the French Revolution," *The New York Review of Books,* 15 February 1990, 49.

16. Auguste Comte, *Physique sociale. Cours de la philosophie positive* (Paris: Herman, 1975), 380-464.

17. For a discussion of Habermas's contribution to the "historians' debate," see Griffioen, "The Metaphor of the Covenant," 531-534.

Auden's poetic observation that "all the real unity commences/ In consciousness of differences" eloquently expresses an insight pivotal to our account of pluralism: real unity can only come from a source that transcends the bounds of human society. Only by becoming aware of the "open heaven" under which society is placed, does it become possible to promote unity without destroying plurality. Christian social thought must provide an account of unity — or, if one prefers, of coherence or solidarity — that does justice to pluralities, whether contextual, associational, or directional. We will briefly outline our own proposals with reference to each of these pluralities.

Contextual Pluralities

It is easy for pluralities, once they are recognized, to become hypostatized — for example, in the form of segregated theologies. This is the "pluralistic contextuality" that, as Max Stackhouse has rightly noted, runs the risk of becoming a "new form of polytheism." The Bible, on the other hand, takes cultural differences seriously without becoming fixated on those phenomena; Paul is ready to become like a Jew to the Jews, but he does so *to win* the Jews (1 Cor. 9:20), to bring them to the knowledge of the One in whom there is neither Jew nor Greek (Gal. 3:28). Not that this "incorporation" would make Jews cease to be Jews. Rather, a new quality is introduced: henceforth one is a Jew *within a body* of which Greeks are also a part. Such is the baptism of the Spirit: all are "baptized by one Spirit into one body — whether Jews or Greeks, slave or free" (1 Cor. 12:13).

Associational Pluralities

The Bible's use of the metaphor of the body has secured associational pluralism an important place in Christian social thought. Just as Paul's injunction in 1 Corinthians 12 and parallel texts, that there "should be no division in the body, but that its parts should have equal concern for each other," has inspired a concern for justice through the centuries, so his teaching that the one body is made up of many parts has fostered an understanding that is perfectly legitimate for the one body to display lasting pluralities. It is no surprise, then, that the idea of associational pluralism has been very attractive to many Christian thinkers.

One cannot mention these themes, however, without being explicit about their inherent dangers. Through the centuries, but especially in the Middle Ages, biblical teaching about the one body and the many parts was unproblematically transposed from the church to society at large. As such, we believe, this is legitimate. The problems arise, however, when the emphasis shifts — as has so often happened — from solidarity between different members to a justification of differences between "higher" and "lower" members. Thus the metaphor of the body has served to sustain social hierarchies. A study of popular preaching in the Middle Ages illustrates the role texts such as 1 Corinthians 12 played in making people accept their station in life within the existing hierarchy: "The social ranks and their respective duties, ordained by God for humanity, were intended to remain fixed and immutable. Like the limbs of the Body, they cannot properly exchange either their place or function."[18] Later on, especially in the 19th and early 20th centuries, the same metaphor lent itself to an organicistic interpretation of society. Here the emphasis shifted from the many parts — preferably conceived as "organs" — to the oneness of the body; as a consequence associational diversity became secondary to the functioning of the whole. It is not

18. G. R. Owst, *Literature and Pulpit in Medieval England* (Oxford: Oxford University Press, 1961); quoted by David Miller, *Social Justice* (Oxford: Oxford University Press, 1976), 282.

surprising, then, that organicist thought in our own century has often shown so little resistance to a (proto-)fascist corporatism that makes the many parts entirely subservient to the well-being of the one *corpus*.

The neo-Calvinist perspective of Abraham Kuyper has been brought to greater clarity on this topic by the Dutch philosopher and legal scholar Herman Dooyeweerd. Dooyeweerd holds that the bodily parts metaphor fails to do justice to the rich fabric of social life. Society does not have the character of an overarching community. To construe society as "a community of communities" is to ignore the irreducible character of various associational spheres — family, church, school, guild, and the like. Such a construal, Dooyeweerd insists, also threatens "free interpersonal relations," that is, relations not contained within specific communities: no one associational sphere by itself "contains" interactions between friends and neighbors, or conversations on trains and planes, or transactions between buyers and sellers or between artists and their audiences. But neither does this mean that individuals are functioning apart from community as such in these in-stances. Dooyeweerd uses the parable of the good Samaritan to illustrate this point. While the Samaritan and the robbed victim were not united in one specific community, the Samari-tan rightly acknowledged an obligation to help. This obligation, which cannot be founded in any one of the distinct communi-ties, nor in society as a whole, can only be understood in the larger context of a community that transcends all specific associational and societal contexts. Dooyeweerd calls this larger context the "supra-temporal community of mankind."

What is true of the "free interpersonal relations" is true of all relationships. They all find their place under "an open heaven." If society is understood as self-contained, without transcendent openness, free relations and community rela-tions will appear to be at odds with one another. Sooner or later someone will attempt to reduce the former to the latter,

170

as happens in organicist thought, or the latter to the former, as in anarchism. Only if the foundation of all human relationships is sought in the "transcendent community of mankind" can we do justice to associational pluralism.

Again Dooyeweerd: "every temporal societal relationship should be an expression of this supra-temporal community, which reveals its full sense in the *corpus Christi*."[19] Note that Dooyeweerd, who is wary of organicism and corporatism, is careful not to associate society as such with the body of Christ. He does affirm, however, that the "transcendent community of mankind" finds its real unity in the *corpus Christi*. In this guarded way he maintains an indirect link between associational pluralism and Pauline teaching about the one body and the many parts.

In Chapter 6 we stressed the important role of "integrative visions." Dooyeweerd is setting forth such a vision, as is Sheldon Wolin in his attempt to avoid viewing associational spheres as a series of "tight little islands"; indeed, even those postmodern philosophers who see society-at-large as nothing more than an "archipelago" of disconnected genres of discourse are offering us an integrative vision of sorts. In a fallen world the attempt to account for the variety of associational spheres will inevitably generate a plurality of conflicting visions. We cannot therefore assess the diversity of perspectives on associational pluralism without recognizing the reality of *directional* pluralism.

Directional Pluralities

Our discussion has at several points focussed on arguments for and against the idea of a "naked" public square. Rawls

19. Herman Dooyeweerd, *A New Critique of Theoretical Thought,* vol. 3 (Amsterdam: Uitgeverij H. J. Paris; Philadelphia: Presbyterian and Reformed, 1957), 582-583.

functioned in our account as the chief protagonist of neutrality. Yet there is room for directional diversity even in Rawls's vision. In his recent publications the "fact of pluralism" has obtained a central place; he does not want to ignore conflicts between "metaphysical, religious, ethical" visions of life. To this extent Rawls challenges the typical liberal attempt to erect a partition between the many private opinions and the one public concern for the common good. However, the thrust of his theory is toward *consensus*. The "fact of pluralism" serves as a test case — is consensus still possible under pluralistic conditions? — rather than as a reality to which justice must be done. Thus his final word on the matter is that the "constraint of publicness" requires a readiness to abstract from ultimate convictions.

In contrast to this account, we have insisted that rival visions cannot be neutralized, either by building a public-private partition, or by constructing an "overlapping consensus." Basil Mitchell has well expressed the objection against such schemes. Neither Christians nor Marxists, for example, can argue that their Christianity or their Marxism should occupy the status merely of a private preference with no authority over our social life and no claim to objective truth. Christianity and Marxism are not "personal ideals" or "profound statements" that can fit happily into the niche that the liberal humanist is ready to provide for them; they are rival philosophies of life.[20]

Here, then, our mood is different than it was in the treatment of contextual and associational pluralism. We want those pluralities to have a lasting place. But it is not so with directional pluralism. The drama being played out in the directional area is much different than in these other two pluralisms.

The Bible places a strong emphasis on the importance

20. Basil Mitchell, *Morality: Religious and Secular,* 54.

172

of directional pluralism. But at the same time it places that plurality in perspective. The directional plurality we witness in the here and now has no ultimate status, since at depth the conflict is a matter of obedience versus rebellion. Hence, instead of focussing on the vast variety of greater and smaller directional differences, the Bible highlights the truly cosmic battle being waged in our world between the diametrically opposed forces of Good and Evil. Viewed eschatologically, only two directions are at stake: obedience and rebellion.

This is a reversal of Rawls's depiction of the situation. Whereas he places unity in the foreground and pluralism in the background, we locate directional pluralism in the here and now, and the unity of life in the eschatological background. On this latter account, however, "foreground" and "background" remain closely linked, since it is the eschatological vindication of the truth that makes it possible for us to accept pluralism in the here and now. In this sense, directional pluralism, too, must be placed "under an open heaven."

CIVILITY AND ESCHATOLOGICAL DELAY

We noted earlier that the eschatological theme looms large in John Murray Cuddihy's case for Christian civility. Basing his proposed Christian strategy for coping with the ordeal of civility on the recognition of the gap between our present imperfection and our future glorification, Cuddihy recommends the adoption of an "ethic for the interim" that prescribes patience as we await God's future victory over the forces of unrighteousness. Christian discipleship, Cuddihy suggests, "puts a ban on all ostentation and triumphalism *for the time being,* before the Parousiatic return, at which time alone triumphalism becomes appropriate and fitting." For Christians to attempt to claim our glory here and now "is precisely vainglory — it is vulgar,

173

empty, and in bad theological taste. 'Whosoever shall exalt himself shall be abased; and he that shall humble himself shall be exalted' (Matt. 23:12)."[21]

There is a way of reading this proposed solution that will see it as a manifestation of uncaring toward the present, thus grounding civility in a kind of Christian cynicism. And there is least a hint of this in Cuddihy's account. In support of his case he appeals, for example, to Glenn Tinder's recommendation that Christians look at the present age with a sense of "resignation" that is outwardly indistinguishable from a "Machiavellian" attitude. But this is not as cynical as it might seem at first glance. Both Tinder and Cuddihy mean to emphasize here the mere *appearance* of Machiavellianism; in reality neither of them is an advocate of the argument set forth in *The Prince*. Tinder is quite explicit on this matter: our Christian resignation, he insists, is only "provisional; and fundamentally it is neither Machiavellian nor ethical, for it is subordinated to a limitless hope."[22]

It is worth asking, of course, whether any kind of "resignation," even a resignation of a highly provisional sort, is an appropriate way of honoring the fact of divine patience. Is civility nothing more than a way of biding our time while we are waiting for the future consummation? Most Christians need to be weaned away from triumphalisms of all sorts, including the eschatologically delayed variety. It would be better to operate with the assumption that the ultimate triumph of sanctifying grace will occur only when we learn that a true triumphalist spirit is not within our human grasp.

Of course, this is not to project an ultimate relativism onto the eschaton — as if Nazism and Marxism and monarchism and Jeffersonian democracy and the politics of apart-

---

21. Cuddihy, *No Offense*, 202.
22. Glenn Tinder, "Community: The Tragic Ideal," *Yale Review* 65, no. 4: 551; quoted by Cuddihy, *No Offense*, 211.

heid will all eventually find their place as pieces in an eschatologically revealed mosaic. We await the revealing of a divine glory whose arrival is rightly thought of as a Day of Judgment.

The posture of public modesty that we are advocating does not presuppose, then, an ultimate synthesis of what are in fact only apparent differences. The conflict is real: truth and righteousness must someday vanquish all falsehood and oppression. The triumph, however, will belong to God. Our appropriate creaturely response to that victory will be one of humble gratitude and not smug vindication.

Moreover, the appropriate response for the present time of the divine patience is the kind of interim public ethic that Cuddihy advocates when he encourages us to limit ourselves politically to the given opportunities for cooperation, accepting the limitations and imperfections of the here-and-now. Such a toleration does not issue from indifference; rather, it is founded on the eschatological certainty that only God can bring about the perfect community.[23]

In our own version of this "interim" public ethics, we are not inclined to draw as heavily as Cuddihy on a communitarian perspective, which highlights the stark contrast between present and future modes of human association. A similar ethic can be spelled out simply by emphasizing the limited nature of politics. The contest between diverse visions of life cannot be decided by political means; politics does not provide us with the resources necessary for adjudicating the conflicting claims that give rise to many of our differences in the public arena. The outcome of such contests can only be awaited. In the meantime, opportunities for political cooperation should be employed as much as possible. As we anticipate the future, let us face the present with a tolerant openness that is not grounded in indifference — whether of

23. Cuddihy, *No Offense*, 209-211.

the Rawlsian variety or some other sort — but is animated by the hope that in the end all that is important to our patterns of public life will be touched by the divine shalom.

To tolerate something, of course, is not to accept it as justified. The tolerance we are prescribing does not rule out a genuine apprehension of the harmful, even destructive, consequences that may well attend the promotion of certain visions of life. What will the ideology of secular liberalism do to the public square? What will result from the inroads of Islam into the free societies of the West? Such questions are important ones. Tolerance does not mean acquiescence.

THE "INNER" CONSTRAINT OF PUBLICNESS

One general advantage of Cuddihy's proposal is that it is motivated by a deep desire to preserve particularities in the process of promoting patterns of public civility. This is an important alternative to the Rawlsian program, which takes it for granted that political toleration and modesty can only be cultivated by rendering particularistic convictions irrelevant to the public arena. As we saw in our exposition of Rawls's case, he is convinced that the constraint of publicness can only occur when we employ abstraction as a means of moving away from specific conceptions of the good.

A Christian interim ethic, on the other hand, can draw on the very particularistic "thickness" that Rawls wants to hide from public view. The Rawlsian scheme fails because it looks primarily for an external public constraint, placing too high a premium on finding public solutions for the dilemmas of public life. Our own case, however, like that of Cuddihy and Tinder, makes much of the way in which a healthy public consciousness must be grounded in an "inner" respect for directional thickness.

Christian conviction is grounded in a particularized

yearning for a new kind of public arena, one that will be on display only when the eschaton arrives. The public square as we presently experience it has to be seen against the background of the eternal horizon of the Heavenly City. For those of us who embrace a partially realized eschatology, it is not unrealistic to expect signs of this City here and now. For example, in a manner not totally unlike the occurrences that Rousseau hoped for in his picnics and parties, we have found something like a public space springing up in the midst of our eating and drinking together in the Christian community. These first fruits of the end time serve both to satisfy and to stimulate our hunger for the concretization of that larger story which, as James McClendon puts it, "overcomes our self-deceit, redeems our common life, and provides a way for us to be a people among all the earth's peoples."[24]

This yearning, in turn, makes us bold to join others in the larger human quest for a healthy public arena, in the hope that on that journey, too, we will experience those mysterious and surprising inklings of a larger kind of love that can take concrete shape — even in the midst of our highly pluralistic here-and-now — in new forms of citizenship and community.

24. James McClendon, *Ethics: Systematic Theology*, vol. 1 (Nashville: Abingdon Press, 1986), 356.

Index

179